JOHN STEWART COLLIS

John Stewart Collis
A memoir

RICHARD INGRAMS

Chatto & Windus

LONDON

Published in 1986 by
Chatto & Windus Ltd
40 William IV Street
London WC2N 4DF

British Library Cataloguing in Publication Data

Ingrams, Richard
John Stewart Collis: a memoir.
1. Collis, John Stewart
2. Authors, English—20th century—Biography
I. Title
828'.91208   PR6053.042Z/

ISBN 0-7011-2976-X

Printed in Great Britain by
Redwood Burn Ltd
Trowbridge, Wiltshire

CONTENTS

ACKNOWLEDGMENTS

I am most grateful to Mrs Irene Collis and Mr Michael Holroyd (Literary Executor) for permission to quote extensively from the writings of John Stewart Collis. I would like to thank them both, in addition, for all their help.

My thanks are also due to the following: Mr Alan Betts (who did a great deal of useful research); Mrs Peggy Burton: Mr Arthur Calder-Marshall; Mrs Elizabeth Coaker; Miss Louise Collis; Dr Robert Collis (Jnr); Mr Sigvart Godeseth; Sir Rupert Hart-Davis; Mr Martin Jenkins; Miss Lilian Kember; Dr David Lawson; Mr and Mrs Dick Merricks; Miss Ruth Pitter; Mr Julian Potter (who provided me with extracts from the unpublished second volume of Stephen Potter's autobiography); Mr Martyn Skinner; the Contessa Terni di Gregori; and Andrew Wilson (whose advice and encouragement were invaluable).

ILLUSTRATIONS on pages 15–18

Frontispiece: John Stewart Collis and Richard Ingrams in 1983.

INTRODUCTION

When Evelyn Waugh wrote a satirical guide to how to get on in the literary world, he advised the would-be biographer that 'If you want to make a success of it choose as a subject someone very famous who has had plenty of books written about him quite recently.'

This is a book about someone who is not very famous and who has had no books at all written about him, though he wrote a very good one about himself. I had not heard of him at all until 1971 when, on a holiday visit to Sussex, I met Dick Merricks, a fruit farmer at Icklesham. He told me how one of his sons had suffered from cerebral palsy and how he had been greatly helped and eventually enabled to lead an ordinary life by a remarkable woman called Eirene Collis, recently dead, who had founded a special unit for the treatment of spastic children at Carshalton. He went on to mention her husband, a writer called John Stewart Collis who, he said, had written about farming and also nature in a memorable way. Always on the lookout for new writers to read, especially those outside the fashionable circle, I made a mental note of the name, and not long after picked up in a second-hand shop a little book called *While Following the Plough*, published in 1947 with wood engravings.

The book is laid out in short sections, each between 1000 and 2000 words long, and is an account of how the author became a farm labourer at the beginning of the 1939–45 war. This is how it begins:

It was 16 April 1940. I could find no lodging close to the farm, but a friend did me the great service of putting me up at her cottage, which was about thirty-five minutes' bicycle ride distance. This meant rising in time to shave, breakfast, sandwich food for the day, and be ready to start out by six-thirty. I had always wanted something to force me up at this hour, this unsmirched hour of promise and hope: and now I stepped out into a clear morning, with frost across the whole land, the air biting and the hollows clouded. I arrived at the farm punctually, trying not to feel nervous and like a new boy at school. I gave up shyness some time ago when I realised that it was a form of self-consciousness and conceit, as well as being, like bad manners, a sign of ignorance of human nature; but to turn up into a completely new milieu – and not looking the part either in person or clothes – to meet employers and employees and do something I had never done before, certainly made me apprehensive.

I expect that was enough to make me interested in the author. He was obviously a good writer – though careless of the finer points of grammar – something of a poet, an opinionated man with a sense of humour. I read on. The little book describes how Collis worked on two farms, one in Sussex, the other in Dorset, and it not only gives a picture of farming life at that time, but also an account of how the author struggled, in the end successfully, to master all the arduous jobs a farm labourer is expected to do, and how in the process his eyes were opened to the business of nature and the extraordinary work of the creation. The writing was alive. There was a feeling almost of exaltation which made it memorable, and made me want to read more of Collis's work. In the years that followed I read most of his other books including *Down to Earth* the sequel to *While Following the Plough*, and his biographies – *The Carlyles*, *Marriage & Genius* etc.

Some years later in 1978 when I was contributing to the *Spectator* I was asked to review Collis's latest and, as it turned out, last book, *Living with A Stranger* – an enquiry into the human body. It was a typically 'Collisian' book, an investigation starting from a position of ignorance into the various bodily organs we carry around with us but never bother to think about except when they go wrong. My review must have pleased him because not long afterwards I received a note in that small, flowery and meticulous handwriting that I came to know so well. 'Have you ever an idle hour, a quarter hour really, to spend at 11 p.m. of an evening?' he asked. 'The BBC, Radio 4, "A Book at Bedtime" are broadcasting extracts from *While Following the Plough* from 6 January to 6 February.' I made a point of listening, although I am normally asleep at that hour. The reader was the actor Alan Badel, an excellent choice. Having himself been an RAF pilot in the Normandy landings, it was fitting that he should end his reading with this passage:

In the day of calamity, in the day of battle, all men must cease from work and rise to slay. All save the ploughman. He must go on. Hence the gesture of that immortal ploughman on the fields of Normandy. When D-Day came and battle raged upon the beaches: when the sky was filled with fighters and the land was lashed with fire, that nameless Man took out his plough and did his work and turned his furrow in the midst of all. And when the brief hurricane of mortal men had passed, he was still there – type of the eternal things, symbol of the sane.

I can remember lying in bed relishing that oratorical prose and feeling the excitement you get from being in close touch with 'the real thing' – poetry, genius, call it what you will.

Some weeks later my wife and I invited ourselves to call on Collis at his house in the Surrey woodland at Abinger Common near Dorking. Why had I left it so late to get in touch with a writer whose work I so much admired? Partly I think because I imagined Collis as an austere and reclusive figure – a man who would not welcome callers. It is always hard to think back to the picture you had before actually meeting someone, especially when, as in the case of Collis, the two images are so very different. In the portrait of him by Sir John Lavery which acts as the frontispiece of his autobiography, *Bound Upon a Course*, he looks a lean and brooding figure, gazing away from the artist with a pensive expression. It was the only picture I had seen, and it had certainly coloured my view. It is only now that I have myself posed with Collis for a photographer and observed the care with which he presented himself to the camera that I can see how calculating he was about the face that he showed to the world: how reluctant he was to be caught off guard, informal and unposed.

So I suppose I approached Park House, Abinger Common, down the narrow sunken road dark with Surrey evergreens, feeling a little apprehensive about the encounter. I could not have been more disarmed by the stocky, ruddy-faced Irishman who almost bounded out to greet us. To begin with he was in no sense an old man, although at the time he was eighty-one. He showed no signs of age. His skin was quite smooth and sun-tanned, his little eyes sparkled and there was a great feeling of

1 John Stewart Collis

2, 3 & 4 John Stewart Collis as a young man, with Bindo in Dorset, and as a farm labourer.

5, 6 & 7 Eirene Joy Collis; John Stewart Collis by Sir John Lavery;
Eirene Collis with patients at Carshalton.

8 & 9 View from Park House, Abinger Common, by Ethelbert White;
John Stewart Collis with his second wife, Irene.

alertness about him. This alertness, or vitality was his most remarkable quality. I was nearly half his age, but he seemed twice as lively, twice as interested in everything as I was. I equate this vitality with genius, some kind of spark that burns more brightly in a select few. Collis always seemed to be in some way more alive than everyone else, which was partly why he found it so difficult to come to terms with the idea of death, or even old age. If he had been told at that first meeting that he had only three years to live he would have been incredulous, as would I. Sadly it was true.

Apart from his superhuman vigour the most noticeable and the most appealing thing about him was his voice. Surprisingly, in view of the fact that he had lived in England nearly all his life, and had even been to public school and Oxford, he still spoke with a strong Irish accent. I realised later that being an Irishman meant a great deal to him and that he always thought of himself as Irish and different from the people amongst whom he had chosen to live. 'The English have a great capacity for not enjoying themselves,' he once said. 'Their lack of exuberance and vitality is remarkable.' His voice was not only Irish, it was soft and beguiling in the way that Irish voices often are. He leant forward. He took you by the arm. Some words were heavily emphasised – just as when writing he frequently used italics, like Cobbett, to stress certain words. My wife, who is also Irish, was immediately charmed by him, as I suspect many other women were. He was courteous and attentive. So far from being austere, Collis was warm and humorous and not in the least bit solemn. We immediately felt that we were friends.

That was in February 1981. When we left we persuaded him

to call in at our house for lunch on his way to Oxford one day in early April when, as he regularly did, he drove to his old college to attend a Gaudy – a reunion with old Balliol men. It was Boat Race Saturday and Collis made a great point of wanting to watch the race on television, so lunch was arranged around this, to him, apparently, unmissable event. However, when he arrived, wearing gym shoes and showing no signs of tiredness after a long, difficult drive, he only watched the race briefly before announcing that the boat race was boring because one always knew after a few minutes who was going to win. We then had lunch and I noticed how easily Collis made friends with our two children. (Only later did I realise how much his own unhappy experiences had made him appreciative of a happy family atmosphere.) Afterwards my wife escorted him to the A34 and pointed him in the direction of Oxford. (Collis, we later discovered, was a reckless driver and had no sense of direction.)

One of the great advantages of being a friend of Collis was that he sent you long letters. He had a small circle of friends and fans who he kept informed of his doings in long, often identically-worded letters. His hero Tolstoy had the same habit. A few days after the Oxford visit we received our first full-length Collis letter:

April 7th 1981

Dear Richard and Mary,

I made it to Oxford with great ease (thank you Mary for being my guide philosopher and friend, for bringing me to the motorway, for 'just up the road' would have thrown me and I would have become faint of heart, e'er I had reached the turning point). The outskirts of Oxford being now totally strange to me I think it was rather smart of me to have worked my way straight to the Martyrs' Memorial via Beaumont Street, and thus to Balliol. I even managed to park my car not far from Blackwell's Bookshop – the windows being entirely full of Malcolm Muggeridge's *As it Was* (sorry if I don't write *Like it Was* – for if he meant 'like' as a joke, it will not be taken as such, now that illiteracy is making such rapid strides).

So to the Gaudy. Vast numbers of white-haired, face-battered Old Men limping across the Quad. I was one of them. And the sight of them put another ten years on my life. Which doesn't leave me far to go. Yet – to set against this was my time with you lot. I reckon, as a rough guess, that tended to *subtract*, say twenty years, from my age. In fact when Mary spoke of the Adults staying at table while the Children went off (or the other way round), I felt quite confused wondering who the children were and who the adults. (I don't much like the word Adults: it is too close to the word Adultery.)

To return to the Gaudy. There was a party in the Master's Lodge at 5.30. Harold Macmillian was there, tremendously sunk in a chair. I went and sat in a chair beside him. He said he had been very ill and nearly died, but had had a voyage on a Container ship which had done him a lot of good. But he said he could not see properly now, not to read. I said – Anyway *you* don't need notes for a speech. He said it was a mistake for him ever to have used notes.

The next stage in the business was a service in Chapel. Then after chapel dinner in Hall. There were 160 guests at the Gaudy. Twenty-six of them were given a place at High Table – and, wait for it, I was one of them! What's more I was facing the hall and so could enjoy the ensemble – the three long tables below, the portraits on the walls of worthies in full regalia and gownery. After the meal, the speeches. First the Master. Then Macmillan. He regained a good deal of vigour once on his feet. In good form – in his melancholy amusing manner. At intervals he paused. That was part of the act, I knew. But at one point he paused for so very long that I became anxious. For a long time he stood there – speechless. Had he lost his line of thought I wondered? A great silence fell upon the hall while still he paused. I knew that he believed in the Pause. But this was going too far. He looked right and left, still speechless. Had he really dried up? Was he really floundering? Was he ill, and would he faint, perhaps fall and be numbered among the congregation of the dead? Waves of silence swept across the Hall: from the floor no coughs, no sound, no murmur. And still the speaker wordless stood: commanding a concentration of attention. Here was true eloquence. Here was oratory unsurpassed. At last he broke the spell, and returned to the lower form of speech. It was the Pause made Perfect . . .

That was to be the first of many such letters over the three brief years that we knew Collis. Obviously he spent a good deal of time writing them which was why, as I now realise, he felt that it was a waste to lavish so much literary effort on one person, and sent the same letter to a number of his friends. There was seldom anything at all personal in any letters he wrote.

We heard from him again about two months later when he was motoring in Scotland:

June 5th 1981

Dear Richard and Mary,

There are no inhabitants in the Highlands. There are sheep however. A lot of them. In twos and threes on every road across the high lands, long, lovely and abandoned save by motorists. But the sheep are not interested in motors, and stride across the road regardless. I am very good at avoiding them as a rule, though once I had to stop, get out, and expostulate with one. 'My dear good sheep,' I said. 'Have you no conception? Can't you respect a moving object? Will you be so kind as to give me right of way?' But it was not impressed, and it was I and not the sheep who turned sheepishly away.

But one day I was less fortunate. At one point we passed an enormous man in a red mackintosh on a bicycle. Later as we sat beside the road for lunch, he passed us and greeted us. Much later on there he was again, unmistakable in a red mackintosh. We decided to wave to him as we passed. But at that moment a sheep crossed the road from his side and my front wheel hit it. At which the enormous man with an *enormous* voice shouted '*You like killing animals don't you?*' and rode on. We stopped to look for the sheep. But it was nowhere to be seen. So we went on. But, some distance away, we could see the man, stationary, and waiting for us. When we came to him, I stopped the car, got out to speak to him. But instead of coming over and yelling at me, he moved off on his bike, turning his head at intervals to shout with his enormous voice – *Murderer!* Presently it was necessary to pass him again, and as we did so he shouted *Dregs!* and followed this up by elevating us to *Scum!*

Some time in 1981 I was asked by Hugo Brunner, then chairman of Chatto and Windus, to contribute to a book called *People*. The idea was for a number of writers to provide profiles of characters, famous or otherwise, who had influenced them or whom simply they admired. To begin with no obvious person came to mind. But then I thought 'Why not Collis?' This was not an idea born out of desperation, for I was under no obligation to contribute to the book; neither was there anything very original about it. A number of critics, notably Bernard Levin and Michael Holroyd, had recently published appreciations of his work. Collis was by this stage quite a well-known figure in the literary world. All the same, I had a strong compunction to write about him which was rather difficult to explain. In fact this was to be the first of three biographical efforts – the second a radio interview for the BBC, and the third this memoir – and in each case I felt the same strong urge, and in each case I can remember when I first had the idea. Collis himself would have put this down to inspiration, a subject we discussed a great deal when I was writing that first profile. Inspiration is thought to affect poets and prophets but not such humble persons as biographers. But Collis was firmly convinced that in writing biography, or even journalism, he relied on it as much as any poet. He could not understand how people could write books or articles to order. One had to be inspired even when writing a review. Not surprisingly, when we talked about writing, it emerged that he was not at all disciplined about his work:

You can hear an author tell you how he works so many hours in the morning, then he has lunch, then he takes the dog for a walk, then so many hours more writing. With me it's a complete shambles! I may spend half the morning looking for some reference which I have lost. I may write for half an hour and then go off to play tennis if I feel like it.

He spent a lot of time just meditating which, even during his second marriage, was not always easy:

'He must not be disturbed'. It is hard for writers to create that respectful attitude. The only way I can create it is to be seen and/or heard typing. Not when I'm looking out of the window searching for my sequence. Not while I'm leaning back, thinking or recollecting or composing. Then I'm fair game to be interrupted. I'm always glad when I can reach for my typewriter and become important again.

Collis had no mock modesty about his writing. He refused to subscribe to the English habit of decrying one's own work. 'I'm not dissatisfied with what I've done,' he said.

I have met authors who've said 'Last night I wrote the most *wonderful* thing and then I looked at it the next morning and I thought, "Oh, how awful, how *ghastly*."' Well it's not like that with me a bit. I write the thing in the evening and I think 'Oh this is simply *frightful*. I can't get it right, I can't,' and struggle away and then I look at it the next day and I find Good God! I didn't realise that I could do it so well. I don't call that boasting exactly.

I used the word genius about Collis in my profile for *People*, which delighted but also rather startled him. He had a high opinion of his own work, but even so 'genius' might be going a bit far. At any rate he never disclaimed the title. Yet there have been times while writing this memoir when I wondered if I hadn't made a mistake. Like familiarity, biography breeds contempt, for it brings under your gaze things which would otherwise remain hidden from all but a tiny handful of people. Collis took more pains than most to conceal certain aspects of himself from public view. His autobiography is full of gaps, instances of dishonesty and evasiveness. As I came to fill in the missing pieces in the jigsaw, they seemed to show him in a tragic and also at times a ludicrous light, quite at odds with my previous conception. Nothing could be more at variance with the dignified façade of the Man of Letters, or further removed from the image I had of him before our first meeting, than the notion of Collis as a figure in a farce skipping agilely away from some irate husband or even father coming after him with a horsewhip. Yet something of the kind is conjured up by this passage in a letter to a friend:

. . . an old enemy, who never forgives a certain weakness of mine, and plays upon it, and who has hit me before, hit me this time, harder than usual, though I said nothing offensive and merely, as is my wont, tried to ignore him and run away. I have succeeded in evading him quite a few times in the past, simply by ignoring his approach. But this time he got into the house when the postman delivered a parcel and I could not get rid of him without a fight.

Pride and vanity lay behind his evasiveness. He refused to bare his soul. Like many Irishmen, he was over-serious and hated frivolity of any kind. He was furious, for example, when John Betjeman, to whom he had sent a copy of *Living with a Stranger* replied 'At present I'm preoccupied with the front at Southend.' All this meant that he could at times be a bore, both as a companion and as a writer. His egotism was as infinitely wearisome as anyone else's. It was an impression I had confirmed for me by his old friend the poet Ruth Pitter. 'I loved him without being in the least bit in love with him,' she told me: 'One did like Collis at sight.' I agreed that this was my own experience. She went on: 'I think everyone did. He always had a fortitude which may have been the result of simplicity or it may have been a little higher. He was a good soldier. The spirits of the woods and fields look after that sort of person because they're closer to nature. God looks after the village idiot.'

'The village idiot'. Ruth Pitter was eighty-seven when I spoke to her – or rather she spoke to me, for she hardly once drew breath – and she kept apologising for her fading memory: 'My evidence is very threadbare, like a dead leaf.' But her categorisation of Collis as the village idiot – how he would have hated it – was one of the things that helped to alter my own view of him, as was her admission that he could on occasion be the most awful bore. All the same, I find that I have come round in a circle and stand by my original description of him as a 'genius'. No one, of course, can quite define what it means. I have already mentioned Collis's abnormal vitality, which seems to me one ingredient. I would add also his own extraordinary faith in himself which sustained him throughout his life. And, again, there is the undeniable fact that his wartime writing has survived for nearly forty years and is now spoken of as a 'classic'.

But I have not written this book on the grounds that Collis was a genius. Nor do I wish even to argue the case for his books. There is no doubt that with the exception of one book Collis was, and still is, a neglected writer. It was a word that his admirers habitually used about him and one which he came to hate. 'If people hear you called "neglected",' he said to me at our first meeting, 'they think to themselves "Very well, let's neglect him some more."' But whatever they themselves may think, there are usually good reasons why authors are neglected. Generally speaking, as Collis himself said of old people who complained of their lot, 'It is their *own fault*.' After *While Following the Plough* and *Down to Earth* the reader of Collis's other books – his biographies etc. – will experience, as I did, a feeling of disappointment. They are all well worth reading, but they are not on the same level. So Collis remains a one book man.* He failed to produce what he hoped posterity would recognise as 'a body of work'.

My own interest in him as a writer, and my affection for him as a person, sprang from his individuality. He was quite unlike anyone I have ever met: certainly he was outside the run of

*Collis's two books, *While Following the Plough* and *Down to Earth*, were later published in one volume with the confusing title *The Worm Forgives the Plough*.

people who make up the literary world. He was not especially clever, and was certainly not an intellectual. He had little interest in politics; he spoke no other language. He belonged to no school. His reading was eclectic, though he had little time for 'modern writing'.

He was an 'original' – a type of person who is becoming more and more of an endangered species. Until his death he retained the enthusiasm of a student, constantly finding new things, new books, new people to interest him. He once wrote to the poet Martyn Skinner, with whom he conducted a long and fascinating correspondence over many years, 'When the progress problem comes up, as it is always doing in one's battered mind, I think of the wonderful people that keep coming into the world.' It is an obvious thought, but not the sort of thing that is often said in these supposedly dark and doom-laden days. Collis's optimism, based on the old-fashioned idea that the world is an exciting and extraordinary place, was irresistible and irrefutable. Now that I know more about his life and all the terrible tribulations he endured, I find that optimism all the more remarkable.

I

The only small service that I performed for Collis during our short friendship was to put him in touch with the *Spectator*. At our first meeting he had just been reading William Gerhardi's posthumously published book, *God's Fifth Column*, and was anxious to write a review of it. Would I have a word with the *Spectator*? I rang Patrick Marnham, who was then the literary editor and who had contributed off and on to *Private Eye* for a number of years. Marnham, I knew, was keen on 'countryside' writers like H. W. Massingham and would be sympathetic to Collis's viewpoint. Collis then rang Marnham, proposing himself as a reviewer in his usual forthright and far from self-effacing manner and although it did not prove possible for him to review the Gerhardi book, he found himself immediately taken on as a reviewer. This was probably due more to Collis's own self-salesmanship than to any recommendation of mine. Journalism in its finished form looks well-ordered and arranged but the reader has little idea of the chaotic conditions in which it is often produced. An editor, if he is any good, has little idea of how his next issue will be filled; and if a man like Collis puts himself forward with certain very definite ideas for articles – so many words by such and such a date – he will often be met with immediate acceptance. Collis was prepared to review any book that was sent to him – his last review for the magazine was an authoritative piece on the memoirs of Luis Buñuel, a man he had never heard of and whose films he had not seen – and he had a very wide knowledge of English Literature thanks to his long years of lecturing for the WEA.

The *Spectator* had had a varying career since the war. In the late Fifties and early Sixties, under the ownership of Ian Gilmour, it achieved a high circulation as well as a reputation for good and lively writing. Then, under other less inspired proprietors, the magazine went down hill, until in 1975 it was bought by Henry Keswick, a City man who had made his fortune in Hong Kong and returned to England looking for ways in which to make himself useful. Keswick installed as editor his old school friend from Eton, Alexander Chancellor – a man about whom little was known at that time apart from the fact that he had worked as a journalist for Reuter's and ITN. He seemed an unlikely choice as editor of the *Spectator*. But it is impossible, or at least very difficult, to tell who will make a good editor. As it turned out, Chancellor – a diffident, charming and shrewd young man who to the casual visitor appeared to work in conditions of complete chaos – became one of the most successful editors in recent times. Under him the *Spectator* was transformed for a few brief years into the most talked-about magazine in the country, though the circulation, it has to be said, never rose far above the 20,000 mark. The received wisdom was that the *Spectator* was 'right-wing', but in fact like all successful journalism it was non-party, taking contributions from people with a wide variety of views, including myself, who supplied a rather idiosyncratic television column for eight years. It was this link that provided Collis with his 'way in'.

Although he had been reviewing for various magazines all his life, he became particularly attached to the *Spectator* and was especially proud to be a contributor. During the last three years of his life book reviewing was his main source of pleasure as a writer. In fact his very first article for the *Spectator*, published on 28 March 1981, was not a review at all but an account of a visit to Mount Etna in 1928. All his life, and especially when he lived alone, Collis had been in the habit of taking off to far-away places on a sudden impulse and usually, as he admitted, in an ill-equipped state. Once during a stormy period of weather in 1974 he decided he had to re-visit Chesil Beach, driving all the way to Dorset from his home in Ewell to stand on the shingle, like King Lear in the storm, relishing the wind and rain and the huge waves: so enraptured was he that he very nearly lost his car to the incoming sea. His visit to Etna was similarly undertaken on the spur of the moment. He had read in the newspaper that the volcano was erupting and that it had engulfed the village of Mascali, and decided that he had to go and see all this for himself. To pay for the fare he sold some letters he had received from Bernard Shaw. A German journalist and some local guides accompanied him some of the way but turned back as they got nearer to the summit. Unsuitably attired in gym shoes Collis continued on up the volcano clutching a handkerchief to his mouth to keep out the smoke until he

dimly saw a stream of grey boiling fluid rising from a cave in the mountain. I approached nearer; and now I heard a noise as of men pouring gravel down a shaft into a ship's hold – sounds of men at work where no men could be at work. I retired through the sulphurous air catching sight while doing so of the chill, fresh snow above. I was satisfied with this.

This was not the only such article that Collis contributed to the *Spectator*. One of the best described his visit to Winston Churchill's lying in state in 1965. In spite of his Irishness Collis had a great love of English state ceremonials – partly perhaps because they brought the English to life. ('There are two occasions,' he once wrote, 'when an Englishman will speak to a stranger in a railway carriage: when the subject of cruelty to animals crops up, and on the Death of Kings.') He had been more enthralled by the drama of the abdication than by any of the political crises of the Thirties; he enjoyed the traditional two minutes' silence in memory of the World War dead and felt most indignant about its abolition. When he heard that Churchill was lying in state at Westminster Hall he felt a strong urge to go and pay homage, calculating that if he left it to the second week of the allotted fortnight and arrived in the middle of the night he would not have to queue for too long. Accordingly he drove up from Ewell arriving at Westminster at 3 a.m., parked his car near Parliament Square, and was pleased to see that there was no queue in sight. 'I walked quickly over Westminster Bridge,' he wrote, 'and turned to the right into Lambeth Palace Road to be confronted almost at once by an enormously wide queue, a long distance from the bridge.'

Collis's heart sank as he joined the queue. Once again he had gone on one of his expeditions without making proper preparations. It was a cold January night and he was wearing only a light overcoat and thin socks. It was unlikely that he would withstand a four-hour wait in the queue:

Something must be done. After we had at last crossed Lambeth Bridge, the queue took an enormous loop round the Green before joining Millbank. In the middle of this Green a marquee had been erected to serve the purposes of a lavatory. I had a hat on and it occurred to me that if I stepped out from my place in the queue, entered the tent, and then emerged hatless from it, I could join the far end of the loop without attracting any notice. And indeed I did accomplish this quite easily.

Collis reckoned that this 'reprehensible tactic' knocked an hour off his queuing time. It was very typical of him to countenance such a trick (he had no qualms about admitting that he had cheated in 'Pass Mods' at Oxford). It was typical of him too to assume that the queuers would somehow not have noticed the hatless man emerging from the marquee and joining their ranks. But the little episode showed Collis's shrewdness when it came to writing journalism. He knew that though his queue-jumping revealed him in a bad light, it made his article more interesting to read.

Collis devoted to all his *Spectator* articles – and especially his book reveiws – an unusual amount of care and effort. But then this applied to everything he wrote. One of the reasons why he did not achieve more in terms of output or success was that he never distinguished in importance between one piece of writing and another. He lavished just as much time and attention on a book review, or even a letter to a friend, as he did on an actual book. Journalism, which to most writers is secondary, something to be dashed off quickly in order to make a bit of easy money, Collis thought of as quite the opposite. He took it very seriously, and hated having to review in a hurry because it prevented him

33

from doing the necessary preparation. He was happiest as, when reviewing a short book about George Orwell by Peter Lewis, he had enough advance notice to re-read several of Orwell's books before writing his piece – not something an average reviewer would think of doing.

In composing his review Collis, quite rightly, attached great importance to the element of surprise and paradox in order to gain or keep the attention of his readers. Likewise he resented any editorial attempts to tamper with his deliberately controversial comments. 'Re that review of mine on Orwell,' he wrote to Martyn Skinner,

don't you think it somewhat strange that though I had said to the lit. editor 'If you want to make the odd change of sentence, won't you consult me first,' and he agreed, nevertheless they mucked about with two sentences. Two that annoyed me. Of course I don't mind this or that of small consequence. But consider (1) I am represented as having written. 'People are often wrong about people.' But I did not write that, I wrote 'People are always wrong about people.' In short I challenge the reader to sit up and take notice and to qualify if he wants to. The other, as printed, is flat (2) I am represented as saying 'Many great writers in their twenties have no character.' But I did not write that. I wrote 'All great writers in their twenties have no character.' Don't you agree it is very annoying to be toned down in this manner as if I don't know my business?

Despite such occasional disagreements, and the fact that he later fell out with the editor, Collis's relations with the *Spectator* remained very cordial. In July 1981 he was invited to the magazine's annual party which was by then established as a major event in the London social calendar. The eighty-year-old Collis described it to his friend Martyn Skinner with all the excitement of a little boy who had been taken out of school for a treat:

I went to a spectacular *Spectator* party at Doughty Street the other day. Such numbers, such a press of people. First person I met was the tall Richard Ingrams, always a pleasant smile or half smile as he keeps a Private Eye on the public scene – very charming really. He introduced me to Sir Robin Day – and I took him up on the danger of being taken at your own evaluation and reminded him that he had said across the Garrick Club general table: 'I'm only a television hack' (I was not being rude. I made it plain that I had been pained at this, since he had done more than anyone else for good TV). He said, 'One must sometimes let slip the truth!' But what can one reply to such a remark as mine, pretty inane at a chance meeting. Then I fell into conversation with Enoch Powell. He had just come from the House – where people had shaken their fists at him, as if he had been the cause of the riots.* However we talked about – punctuation in literature. The Greeks, he insisted, like modern lawyers, eschewed punctuation. Only the full stop. Were we then supposed to learn something from the Greeks under this head? I asked. But I did not hear his answer because of the throng which engulfed us. I ran into Auberon Waugh and muttered my name. 'Dr Collis?' he asked. I could not think what he meant;† and supposed that he reads only his own articles in the *Spectator* and I passed on. I was introduced to Anthony Howard, editor of the *Listener*. Disappointing. He didn't say Yes to a remark but 'Yah, yah,' while gazing across the room. I pushed away. Ah, enter Michael Holroyd with attachment. Always the same tall charming self, but not one to hold converse with at a party. I never attempt it. Is Alexander Chancellor the editor present, or rather which is he? 'Over there.' I

*The Brixton race riots of summer 1981.
†Waugh may have been thinking of Dr Collis Browne, inventor of the well-known cough linctus.

went and had a word with him. Good-looking man. Very cordial to me. Much struck with my article on the Grand Canyon. Great honour to have me on the paper. That's better, I felt. The throng became thicker and thicker one could not move save by inches . . . Then I met Patrick Marnham, the lit. editor. Another tall and good-looking chap. Pleasant exchanges. 'Can I go over the 900 words with my Tolstoy?' I asked. 'Yes, 1400.' This was the main question I had hoped to ask . . . A good party.

As far as I remember, Collis's main interest in me during this summer of 1981 was to get me to use my influence with the *Spectator* to become its Wimbledon correspondent. ('Do you think Chancellor could procure me a press ticket? Would you ask him? I don't much like asking him myself . . .') All his life Collis had been mad about tennis and continued to play very well even when over eighty. His idea of heaven was to sit in the Centre Court at Wimbledon. Unfortunately in 1981 my request came too late; the press ticket had already been allocated to someone else. The following year, however, he was luckier, and got his ticket. Collis was absolutely thrilled. He wrote to Skinner:

> Centre Court Press Stand
> All England Lawn Tennis Club
> Wimbledon
> June 23 1982

What price present address? The Fact is I've got from the *Spectator* a Press Pass ticket for Wimbledon. Imagine then my situation. On my left the Royal Box, full of Princes and Princesses and Dukes and Duchesses. Just below me various Players, plus Sue Barker being consoled by Cliff Richard. To left and right some truly fearful Fleet Street faces.

It was a great relief that Wimbledon came after the Falklands War. For it was so unbearable. Young men dying, actually being killed, not for a cause but for Clause 502. As for preventing future 'aggression' and upholding International law, it won't have the slightest effect. That is complete humbug.

The main talking point at Wimbledon that year was whether McEnroe would beat Connors in the Men's Singles. Because of his childish behaviour on court, McEnroe was unpopular with the commentators and the crowds, but Collis defended him: 'His character is awful indeed – but if we are to judge artists by their characters – where will that lead us?'

Even so, he did not think that McEnroe would win. 'His gifts will avail him nothing this year,' he wrote,

For Connors stands in his way. He is not as resourceful as McEnroe, but he will bend him to his will. His mind and character will overpower McEnroe. Watch him forever fingering his racquet between rallies, then bending over it like a scholar examining a corrupt text: it is clear that he is in command of the situation however black it may seem at times. This year he will overcome McEnroe as he did Alexander and regain the title.

Unfortunately this entirely accurate prediction, made when McEnroe was the general favourite, did not appear in the *Spectator* before the result was known. 'An awful thing happened,' Collis told Skinner.

I wrote as requested an article which should have come out on the day before the men's final. I predicted the winner – and gave the same reasons as Rex Bellamy in the Times *after the event*. I sent it in in good time. The editor was too incompetent to put it in on that day (for it would have been good journalism, would it not, win or lose?) I let them know my feelings . . .

(Collis did not say so but almost the same thing had happened in 1977 when he wrote a piece on Wimbledon for *Radio Times* predicting, again accurately, not only that Borg would win the men's finals but that Virginia Wade, an outsider, would be Women's Champion. For whatever reason, this part of his article was omitted.)

The following year, 1983, Collis was again commissioned to cover Wimbledon for the *Spectator*, and again he was determined to predict the winner. After the debacle of 1983 everyone was keen to make amends. Alexander Chancellor confessed to him that he had spent sleepless nights following his failure to print the previous year's article in time. This year special arrangements were made to meet the deadline. Collis, who had sat up half the night writing his piece, drove up from Abinger to London to deliver it in person. It took him one and a half hours to reach Doughty Street where he was personally received by Chancellor and was offered coffee and a sofa to lie down on and rest. The article duly appeared the following day predicting that Lendl would beat McEnroe in the semi-final and then go on to win the championship. It was wrong. McEnroe won.

It was very typical of Collis's bad luck in such matters that the only one of his three Wimbledon predictions to be printed should have been inaccurate.

Collis could never forgive Chancellor for his failure to print the original prediction and had a low opinion of him ever afterwards. In addition he took a poor view of his apparent

38

reluctance to publish an article on coral which he had written following a visit to his nephew Robert in Jamaica in 1972. It was submitted and accepted and Collis was told that the editor liked it. But the months went by and the coral article did not appear. Collis, who never understood the ways of editors, became more and more baffled and perplexed. After nine months during which there was still no sign of the article, he decided to remonstrate with Chancellor. As he told Martyn Skinner:

I rang. He was 'busy'. 'Shall I ring back?' 'Yes, please.' He did not. Being a persistent person I rang again next day. Spoke to Jenny, his sec. I explained to her what it was about, and she said, Yes, he did intend to put the article in. I have since regretted not saying 'Well, Jenny' – for I made contact with her at the Spec. party – 'If he has not the good manners to speak to me for three minutes or write a line, I'm too young to teach him manners.' Not much point I suppose in saying that since she could not repeat it. But it 'raised the Irish in me', as they say . . .

Luckily for Collis, by this stage he had acquired a new ally at the *Spectator* in the shape of Andrew (A.N.) Wilson, who had been appointed literary editor in 1982. Almost alone of the *Spectator* staff during the three years that he wrote for the magazine, Andrew saw the point of Collis, realised his genius and became one of his greatest admirers and best friends. Like many writers, Collis could be a very demanding man. He flattered himself on his Irish shrewdness in dealing with people, but he could never understand why it was that editors and publishers might not wish to have long conversations with him on the phone whenever he chose to make himself available. In his obituary, published in the *Spectator* in March 1984, Andrew Wilson wrote that when they first met, Collis reminded him of the Ancient Mariner not only because he was 'lank and brown – brown as a nut and glowing with strength and health' but because he had an apprehension that Collis was going to waste his time, adding that, in the event, 'We spent many hours talking to one another, on the telephone, or in pubs, or best of all, out in the sunshine. But not a second of that time was wasted.'

Collis, so long accustomed to rejection and rebuffs, to begin with found it difficult to accept that in Andrew he had a devoted and disinterested admirer. Like an animal that has been maltreated he shied away from the proffered hand of friendship. He was even envious of Wilson's success as a writer complaining to Martyn Skinner 'He is an extremely nice man. But in a literary struggle way, he has not struggled and may never have to struggle, and may never realise what people like you and me had to go through.' Such a remark showed how, for all Collis's surface bonhomie, the years of neglect never ceased to rankle. Nor could he quite accept that Andrew Wilson's admiration and affection were completely disinterested. When Andrew sent him a note congratulating him on one particular book review Collis could still not accept it without reservation. 'An older man would not have thought it politic to write,' he told Skinner, 'lest I take advantage in some way, a fuss about cuttings and corrections, demands for a little more space, all sorts of things.' It never crossed his mind that Andrew Wilson, however young or old, would not have in the least minded being subjected to such demands from someone he so much admired. Why, he was even prepared to take up the cudgels on behalf of the famous coral article, which was finally printed, in the absence of the editor on holiday, in the summer of 1983.

II

Normally in a short memoir of this kind it would not be thought necessary to dwell at any great length on the early years. However, in Collis's case his childhood was in one major respect so unusual that something must be said about it; for it is not too much to claim that it affected the whole of his life in a profound way.

Collis was one of two twins, John and Robert, born in 1900. His father was a successful solicitor, W. Stewart Collis, of Collis and Ward, 13 Clare Street, Dublin. Both his grandfathers had been well-known Dublin surgeons, but his father's father cut his finger while operating in the days before anti-sepsis and died within forty-eight hours. Collis's father was thus left at the age of twenty with little or no money. But, according to Robert Collis, 'so strong was he that he combined working in a lawyer's office as an apprentice, his law schools in Dublin University and Rugby football with such effect that he not only got the gold medal in the law school but won his cap for Ireland at the same time.'

The Collises were pillars of the Anglo-Irish bourgeoisie – the 'quality' as they were referred to by the natives. They lived in Killiney, a semi-suburban resort on the coast of County Wicklow, in a large house called Kilmore; overlooking the sea and complete with grass tennis court, croquet lawn and stables. Despite the unhappiness in his family Collis always loved this

43

place and in later life he returned to Ireland whenever he could, finding in the surrounding countryside and especially in the Wicklow Mountains the solace of that peculiar and bewitching atmosphere that never seemed to change.

'Indeed I find today,' he wrote in 1971,

everything everywhere is exactly as it always has been. The same sparseness of inhabitants; the same air of desolation; the same expanse of empty acres browned or purpled by heather, and the darker spaces that keep moving because they are not made of heather but of cloud shadows; the high haycocked field on a green hill far away, upon which alone the sun is shining; the all-pervading silence emphasised by the bleating of one sad sheep out of sight; here and there great boulders perched on the top of eminences, and granite rocks sinking ever lower into the heather; the abandoned bogs; the recurrent rainbows seldom complete in their archways, and more often as pillars not in the sky but set against a verdured hill or mountain crest; the white cottage discerned at the foot of the dark mountain, Image of Loneliness . . .

John (Jack) and Robert (Bob) were the youngest of a family of five – Maurice, who later became a well-known writer, and two sisters, Mary and Joyce. Maurice was eleven years older than Collis and when they were young the brothers saw little of one another. 'Maurice was the clever boy of the family,' Collis wrote after his death,

good passes at examinations. First in history at Oxford, then Indian Civil Service and District Magistrate of Rangoon. Retired in 1935 to take up new career as author, starting with *Siamese White* which was an instant success. All his books are good, most enthralling – except the last ones which Bob and I took a very dim view of.

Collis saw as rivals his elder brother, and to some extent his twin Robert, who published a successful memoir, *The Silver Fleece*, in 1936 – a feeling that was apparently reciprocated by Maurice. 'I always praised Maurice's books quite elaborately to him,' Collis wrote to Martyn Skinner,

though he took all the limelight. But when my *Bound Upon a Course* was acclaimed, he was pained. As I was not successful with the books for which I am now acclaimed, he only gave perfunctory interest. But he didn't like to see me catching up, and he would certainly not have been able to bear my dark horse win after the loneliness of the long distance runner.

What marked Collis off from the rest of his family and most of the rest of mankind was the attitude of his mother. The daughter of a Dublin surgeon, she had been pronounced delicate by her father and from then on was indulged by her parents. Originally they had opposed her when she said she wanted to marry Mr Collis, a mere solicitor, so she shut herself into her room for a week, after which they relented. But, like her parents, she soon came to despise her husband and his middle-class ways. How she hated his bridge parties, which she did her best to wreck by serving horrible teas. All her life she was prone to tantrums, and all her life no one saw fit to restrain her. She had already given birth to three children, and neither she nor her husband was pleased when she became pregnant again, this time with twins. She had a difficult confinement and was given a sedative with the result that the second child, Robert, was born in a rather drugged state. After a struggle he at last began to breathe and was handed to his mother. The first born twin, John, was

45

forgotten and hardly looked at for several days. 'From the hour of my birth she hated me,' Collis wrote. 'The earliest years were so difficult to take that I have suffered virtual loss of memory.' Many years later, he said, he came across a photograph of himself at about the age of two. 'I was utterly amazed to see quite a normal child that must have run across a room, fallen over, burst into tears, run to its mummy and been comforted in the normal way. But that never happened to me. I was never taken up in my mother's arms and kissed . . .'

Perhaps there was something about Jack that reminded her of her poor husband. All her affection went on Bob, the twin. She said goodnight to him, but not to Jack; she read stories to him, but not to Jack; she gave him a second helping, but not to Jack – 'all the sorts of things,' Collis said, 'that are like *a thousand knives* stuck into one at that age.' If he tried to have it out with her she would only say 'How dare you speak to me like that in my house?' or, if accused of lack of love, 'Of course I love you.' What was even more extraordinary was that Mrs Collis would visit one of her sons, but not the other. Only when she was very old and dying in a Dublin nursing home did her attitude soften and she seemed for the first time in her life pleased to see her son:

'I was glad to sit with her,' Collis wrote,

for it was a relief to be able to do so without tension and without pain. She had never looked straight into my face before, nor had I looked directly at her. Only one thing was I resolved upon – I did not favour a death bed reconciliation. It was too late for that. Moreover I am so easily mollified that I feared falsity on my part. But I could see it coming. And sure enough one day I found her preparing to try for this. 'There is something I want to say to you,' she began. I looked alarmed

'Here goes,' I said to myself. 'There is something I want to say to you,' she began again. But I would not yield. I would not soften. I would not depart from my resolve. I did not let her continue, but bending over the bed, lightly and swiftly stroked her cheek and said 'It doesn't matter, mother, say nothing.' She did not try again and I think she was relieved . . . I am persuaded that I was right and used good sense on this occasion. It was quite beyond her to have employed words to deal with this matter without deception, and beyond me to have listened seriously and responded sincerely. If, in a vague way, before passing from the face of the earth, she sought forgiveness, I thought it best that it should be done without words, and in fact I believe that she saw in my action all that she needed without the necessity of either of us uttering a single sentence.

Why Collis's mother acted as she did is impossible to explain. There was no logical reason for her hatred. What made it worse for him was that the issue was never discussed in the family. He was never offered any explanation as to why he should be treated differently from other children. It was not until he was nineteen that anyone saw fit to mention the matter. Then a dying aunt summoned him to her bedside and told him 'It sometimes happens that when a mother has two sons at the same time, she will adore one of them and hate the other. I thought it might relieve and comfort you to know this.' In fact it was such a relief to him that years later he could remember his aunt's exact words.

His brother Robert, who became a celebrated paediatrician, gave him a similar message when Collis showed him the manuscript of his autobiography, *Bound Upon a Course*, which contains a full and fascinating account of his childhood: 'This is a very common psychological matter which I meet all the time as

47

a children's physician – among the primitive Africans it is common to find a mother who gives all her milk to one and literally lets the other one die.' Not wanting the family dirty linen to be washed in public Robert was keen for his brother not to make too much of his mother's rejection. Yet for Collis, it was not something that could be brushed aside in an anthropological footnote.

All the same the remarkable thing was that he survived. For this he had his nature to thank, which was always sunny, tolerant and equable. Had it been otherwise he might have developed into a neurotic personality: but there was never the smallest trace of any morbidity in him and the fact that he bore no grudge towards his mother is in itself proof of his remarkable lack of malice and his naturally conciliatory and loving temperament. In some ways, as he himself maintained, his childhood experience may even have been beneficial. 'I don't say she didn't harm me,' he told me, 'she harmed me very greatly, but she strengthened me, and above all she gave me a *twist*, an inner *twist* without which I don't think I would have been able to write the books.' I never asked him to define what he meant by the 'twist', but I think in general what he was getting at was that, as with other writers who have been unhappy in childhood, that unhappiness acted as a spur to becoming a writer. It was certainly true that Collis's character was strengthened by his mother's indifference. It made him, he said 'extraordinarily self-sufficient'. Though highly sensitive, he developed a marked degree of detachment which enabled him to cope with all the other varieties of neglect which were to befall him in later life – neglect by wife and children, by publishers, by critics, by the public. He never asked for help, never invited pity. In the most extraordinary and exceptional way he was able to endure year after year of failure and survive without becoming bitter.

One other, less beneficial effect was to make him very ambitious. 'Up to the age of thirty,' Collis said, 'there is no desire so strong as the desire to prove to a sceptical family that you are a long way its most distinguished member.' More so, he might have added, if you are the Cinderella of the story. All three Collis brothers were very competitive, but because of his status Jack was desperately eager to distinguish himself. 'Ambition,' he said, 'is rarer than is often supposed. The family idol loves to shine much more steadily than the English sun, but he is not filled with a burning ambition to do so since his light is already so luminous. It is the non-spoilt children who build empires and found dynasties . . .'

Collis had no memory of anything that happened to him before the age of nine. He blamed his mother for the fact that he was so backward. He couldn't remember ever learning to read or write. 'I was a very slow developer,' he said, 'and that may have made me slower, may have made me look inwards too much.' Everything suggests that his character developed quite independently of outside influences, with the possible exception of Irish nannies. He grew up inside a cocoon. One of the strangest things about him was that he bore no traces of his education. It was not only his accent that remained obstinately Irish; his attitude to life, to people, was quite unaffected by the public school and Oxford ethos, which normally has so marked an effect on those who go through the system. His twin brother, Collis Major at Rugby, was very different. Energetic, sociable and boundlessly self-confident, he threw himself into public school life, becoming an excellent Rugby player like his father and an all round sportsman, exactly the type of athletic young man that Frank Buchman was keen to recruit into his Moral Rearmament movement, with which he flirted for a time. He went on to become a paediatrician with a worldwide reputation and many of the characteristics of the successful hospital consultant – drive, bombast, impatience, but also charm, vitality and good humour. Collis Minor, though never at all an 'outsider', had no such success. 'I was a perfectly *hopeless* schoolboy,' he told me. 'I found it very hard to pass any examinations. I didn't feel I had any particular gifts. I had *no* character. *No* self-esteem.' Any lack of self-esteem was, again, due to his mother. For whatever harm she did him, and he admitted that she did him considerable harm, was caused by the feeling that he must be in some way to blame for her dislike of him. Neither his brother nor his sisters, he said, understood the relation between him and his mother. They were apt at intervals to moralise at him, hinting at a lack of love on his side. It would be impossible for a small boy in that situation not to think that he had done something to deserve his treatment, to wonder what sin he had committed, still more so if the rest of the family seemed to condone the mother's behaviour: never trying to explain it, never offering sympathy or consolation. The boy would naturally assume that there was something the matter with him, something so serious, so ineradicable that it could not even be referred to. I never discussed this aspect of his story with Collis and he never referred to it – though I think he did say once that as a child he had felt 'ashamed', especially when strangers

50

came to the house. But I think that for all his apparent self-confidence he never wholly lost that feeling of inferiority or ever gained that missing self-esteem which he observed in himself as a schoolboy. It was noticeable that even when he was old and, in worldly terms, successful, he had a continual craving for reassurance and for praise. He minded too much if his books or his articles were ignored. He desperately wanted to receive flattering notices and fan letters – to be told that he was good. I remember being struck at our first meeting by this. I had expected to find a man who was secure in his own fame, two of whose books had sold in their thousands and one of which was recognised as a classic. What should I be to him? Just a visiting journalist, one of many perhaps, who admired his work and came to offer homage. Instead I found that my enthusiasm for his books meant an enormous amount to him. He was just as delighted to meet me as I was to meet him. This response was in its way very touching, and to me flattering. But in a sense it lessened him in my eyes, the more so when I came to know him better and realised how much he depended on compliments and praise. Every writer has that dependence to some extent. But in a man of Collis's age and achievement it was undignified. I felt that now he was over eighty he ought to be concerned with more important things than what people thought of him. It was partly due to his failure to attain a spiritual indifference to the opinions of the 'world' – easy enough to talk about but not so easy to acquire – but I think now that it was also a throwback to his childhood and that he was, and had always been, a little boy who felt aware and ashamed of some unspoken inadequacy on his part, and who could never have enough attention and reassurance to make up for it.

III

Collis says little about his father in his memoirs, but he was a kind man and it was thanks to his help – he gave him an allowance of £150 a year – that he was able to 'become a writer'. He might have pursued other careers. At Oxford, where he went after a short spell of military training, he read English at Balliol. 'There was no doubt Jack was different from my Merton brotherhood,' his best friend Stephen Potter wrote. 'In spite of Rugby he was not so safe and sound and public school as we were. Was it his caustic Irishness? He was ambitious.' Collis had little time for his lectures and instead spent many happy hours at the Union taking part in debates, an enthusiasm that usually turns young men towards politics. But he was never really interested in the Issues of the Day, simply bewitched by the power of oratory. He was fascinated by the many visiting speakers and studied their techniques, occasionally spellbound, as when W. B. Yeats came down to Oxford to debate the Irish question. It was an interest that he sustained all his life, and in one of his best *Spectator* pieces he voiced his outrage on discovering that politicians employ speech writers instead of doing it themselves. A letter to his first wife describes the famous Scottish Socialist James Maxton:

A wise instinct took me to hear Maxton. He was very good. Once again – can you believe it? – I heard a great man making a great speech; even now in 1931. It was a very crowded meeting and I stood not on a chair but on the back of a chair. It was the most remarkable meeting. Fabians. Bourgeois to the end of their fingers. The secretary, robust, bright red-face, exactly right. Enter Maxton with his dark suit, pale green face, enormous head, tremendous black hair, revolutionary features. He speaks for one hour. He *says something* all the time. But what does he say? He says very politely but with absolute clarity that the Fabians are complete asses, that evolution in socialism is a trick word to prevent revolution, that the Labour Party has done nothing in Parliament and a great deal besides. I have never heard a man be so good-humouredly insulting to an audience. Insult after insult, but with such mock humility, such wit.

Collis's love of oratory also attracted him to the Church, and he spent a short time at a theological college immediately after leaving Oxford. But the influence of Bernard Shaw, whose play *John Bull's Other Island* had electrified him when he saw it in Dublin at the age of sixteen, was stronger than any of his religious inclinations. He set out to write – and vowed to begin by writing a book about his hero Shaw. So he went to London and rented a room at the back of a pub in Rotherhithe Street overlooking the river and Wapping – 'Rotherhithe Street – street of warehouses, of recurring pubs, of watery glimpses, unearthly street. Silent, empty, cobbled, cliffed-in path by day: by night a greater silence on the gleaming filthy stones, an echoing chasm where no mountains are – a gorge lit up by lampposts.'

He didn't mix with the East-Enders, which is surprising in view of how well he later got on with his fellow farm-workers. Locally, perhaps, he was thought of as an eccentric. He had been told, for example, that no sane man would swim in the

Thames, yet one summer evening he took it into his head to plunge into the river. Once when there was a fire in one of the nearby wharves, realising that he could only see it from the river, Collis swam out again and was engulfed by a mass of melted rubber, returning to the shore blackened from head to foot. He loved to perform such acts of dare-devilry. He rode his bicycle across the frozen Serpentine watched by an incredulous police-man. He ran through the streets of London pursued by taxi-drivers who thought he must be trying to catch a train. Some-times on summer evenings he would catch a train out into the countryside, throw off his clothes and run for five miles without stopping. He particularly liked going to Chesil Bank in Dorset, where his friend Middleton Murry had a coastguard cottage which he rented to Collis for long periods. Here he would sit for hours gazing out to sea, imagining he was on a ship or again, on impulse, hurling himself into 'the most dangerous bay in Eng-land':

Every year people were drowned there. The difficulty was not in the under-current but in the immediacy of the shelving and the ferocity of the backwash. Once out it was very hard to get on the shore again if the waves were high. The swimmer was knocked down and dragged back without being able to get a footing . . .

Nevertheless I preferred swimming when it was rough than when it was only moderately rough. I liked a good wave; the sensation of mounting a perpendicular hill, passing over the crest and sweeping into a valley while the shore disappeared from sight, then up again and over another, was worth the difficulty of getting back.

It was a pleasure that could be overdone. When it was getting near the time of my departure for London I was treated to a succession of wonderful seas. They were very tempting. One day when there was absolutely no one about (Middleton Murry away) the waves grew better and better and I determined to have a swim. It was about seven o'clock in the evening. I went down to the shore and stood for a long time looking at the waves. It was terrifying. Half an hour passed as I looked on, while I became more and more afraid of being a coward. Three quarters of an hour passed and I no longer had the courage to draw back. And I felt it would be a first-class experience of aloneness and isolation . . . So I dashed in and soon was mounted on white horse after white horse. But the moment I got there all ideas of enjoying isolation immediately vanished and I was filled with but one thought – to reach the shore again. Though I had gone out the shortest possible distance behind the break of the waves the shore was miles away. Long terrific rolls of wave separated me from a foothold on the pebbles; and the crashing and breaking up of the waves on which I was perched in succession occurred long before any such foothold could be obtained. I had learnt how to choose my wave upon which to start on the desperate dash to the shore. The property of the chosen wave was that no big one followed it for a bit. On this occasion the choice was of desperate importance, for if I made a mistake and chose a wave that was followed by another immediately it would be a bad look-out. I remained stationary for a long time attempting to choose. But every wave was followed by two or three others of ferociously frothing appearance. Yet a choice had to be made. I chose at last a very big one swelling with pride of place and apparently followed only by lowly satellites. Mounting on it and swimming shorewards I felt its embrace at first behind and then saw it in front, at which moment it suddenly fell to pieces. All support gone I fell also and was thrown about underneath as if I weighed no more than a stick. I felt the bottom for a moment, got a footing but was driven backward in the wash, and looking up saw one of the supposed satellites now swollen to a greater monster than the former, and which, clawing the sky above them, collapsed over me. I

56

left the ground, was lifted up, thrown backwards into what felt like the centre of the ocean and jerked forward high on the beach. To escape with only a headache seemed creditable. But that was my last essay in wave mountaineering.

Collis stayed in his Rotherhithe room for eighteen months in a state of Bohemian squalor. 'Jack had an extraordinary indifference to physical comfort,' his friend Stephen Potter wrote:

His bed was never actually made from one year's end to another – the blankets were just pulled up in one tug. He would never do anything to improve or smarten up his room, never buy a shilling pot of paint. There was never a moment when every plate and glass was washed up. The sight of a typewriter standing orderly seemed to inspire Jack best if it was isolated in the midst of a sea of wreckage. The shocking old seagull on the pile outside, the banks of low-tide sludge beneath his window, the crumbs and cigarette ash on the carpet, all helped his concentration. In the midst of muddle Jack was clear and crisp and eloquent.

Potter, who later achieved worldwide fame with his *Gamesmanship* books, was Collis's best and closest friend. They had been at Oxford together, and were bound by their love of literature and a shared sense of humour. Both were would-be writers.

'They were careful to exchange inter-literary compliments,' Collis wrote in his unpublished novel, *Progress of an Artist*:*

though neither took the other's work very seriously. Stephen had a vague feeling that Jack was bound to be successful, might at any moment suddenly surpass himself and leap upwards: but that was only

*Although written in fictional form, this book is barely disguised autobiography – I have here changed the names back to their originals.

57

a dim irritation, and having no sense of destiny in himself nor understanding it in others, Stephen didn't take it to heart. And if at any moment he felt a pang of envy towards Jack he would say so loudly – instead of ticking him off. Jack enjoyed watching the way in which Stephen made the best of living, always managing to dress well, to go to cocktail parties and cinemas, to play golf and tennis, to drive motor cars, without being able to afford it . . . They could discuss any topic, confess any sin sexual or otherwise, admit any ignorance or faux pas without fearing the slightest eyebrow raising. 'What exactly does the disestablishment of a church mean?' Jack would ask, for instance, or confess 'I have no idea at all what Napoleon III *did*.' And Stephen who delighted in the extraordinary fields of ignorance he was always coming across in Jack would enlighten him if he could.

Both Collis and Potter had fallen under the spell of G. B. Edwards, a writer who was totally unknown until recently, when his novel *The Book of Ebenezer le Page* was published post-humously. Edwards was a critic who, like Collis, lectured in English history and drama for the Workers' Educational Association and also at Toynbee Hall. 'He suffered throughout his life,' Collis wrote in an epitaph which could just as well have been his own, 'from three terrible things: poverty, publishers and women.' Although he was an exact contemporary, Potter and Collis revered him as if he was a much older man – but later they fell out with him when they could no longer stand his constant scrounging.

'To Stephen Potter and myself he seemed always a genius,' Collis wrote in a long review of the Penguin edition of *Ebeneezer* in the *Spectator*:

He was the most dynamic character we had ever met. To be dynamic may mean no more than to be fully alive; but he had something to say, he spoke from an inner-centre, as one having authority and not as the scribes and pharisees. He had dark hair, a good forehead, marvellous teeth, very brilliant eyes shining with intelligence and warmth – but a sloppy indeterminate mouth. He reacted to life almost with an animal's lack of calculation. He was really *affected* by people he met, and made little attempt to conceal his version of their character. Introducing him to someone was like conducting a chemical experiment. If he found the person alien to his taste, say an intellectual sophisticate, he would be unable or unwilling to conceal his reaction. He would grow pale. He would not only lower his eyes but his whole head slanting his face away from the person. He might not say anything at all, only bow his head still lower . . .

Since Johnson's Savage, the unrecognised genius who lives on only in the tributes of his disciples has become a familiar character in literary biography. I doubt if Edwards ever deserved the high praise that Collis lavished on him. His importance here is that it was thanks to his influence that Collis went the way he did and struck out on his own. Collis's first book, a short study of Bernard Shaw, had been published in 1925 when he was twenty-five. It was remarkable for the confidence and boldness with which it was written. The book was very well reviewed and reprinted twice. Sean O'Casey wrote to him: 'It is in my opinion a brilliant book and though I don't agree with everything you say, I believe it to be worthy of the great man you write about and that's saying something.' No young writer could have got off to a more promising start.

But then Jonathan Cape suggested to Collis that he should follow up his *Shaw* with a book about St Paul. This seems to have been one of those suggestions that are made by publishers off the top of the head. After Bernard Shaw, why not St Paul?

They were both famous and influential figures, each with a large following. Collis, however, turned the offer down. It had never crossed his mind, he said, that he could be given a subject. Whatever he wrote must be the result of a 'colossal inner compulsion'. His friends could not understand him. One of them drew his attention to the case of the poet Edward Thomas who had written several books – travelogues and biographies – simply to make money. But Collis would have none of it. He absolutely refused, he said, 'to join the ranks of the "little famous" – to use Keats's perfect phrase. I refused to write books of the same nature but waited to be propelled by the fire within.'

So to the alarm of his parents and the despair of his friends he turned his back on a conventional literary career. He was not going to undertake commissions, he refused to do a part-time job. Instead he would write – but only what he wanted to write; not what someone else wanted or what might earn him some easy money. It was a brave and foolhardy decision, but without it Collis would never have done what he did and it is doubtful if today anyone would have heard of him. He was helped to make it by his sense of vocation: 'He had an inkling' – he wrote of himself in his novel – 'that he was destined in some way – but how feeble was that inkling. It was less than a whisper, far thinner than a still, silent voice. It demanded obedience, but it gave little help and promised no triumph.' And again: 'Something inside him, about the size of a seed, far away in a corner, made him silently decide that rather than be a member of what Keats called "the little famous" he would be a great failure.' He had no idea what was involved. Like all the major decisions in his life this one was taken blindly and impulsively – 'burning his boats, almost without knowing it'.

How different his life would have been had he set to and written the book about St Paul. He might have become a successful literary figure, well known in the corridors of Broadcasting House, his name familiar to the readers of the fashionable weeklies. That Collis chose to go his own way was due much to the influence of G. B. Edwards, a non-compromiser if ever there was, who no doubt instilled the lesson that Collis must be propelled by 'the fire within' before he could write anything worthwhile. The only snag was that at this stage Collis had no special fire within to propel him. Certainly Edwards was unlikely to provide it. Like many unrecognised geniuses he was very good at demolishing everyone elses's work but not so good at constructing something of his own. Collis was determined that before he could do anything worthwhile he must first provide himself with a satisfactory creed. Philosophy, religion, politics – all these things must be made to make sense. Edwards was influential in diverting Collis away from his idol Bernard Shaw and collective solutions to human problems. But what he offered him in place of his false prophets was not a very nourishing brew. Under his guidance Collis immersed himself in Walt Whitman, Havelock Ellis and Edward Carpenter and in the process he became the devotee of a kind of watered-down nature worship which was very fashionable in the 1920s. The study of nature became a substitute for religion, *Leaves of Grass* replaced the New Testament. Collis wrote a little play called *Forward to Nature* (1927) in which the hero preaches the need for a rediscovery of nature. It was a complete failure. He tried a novel, *The Sounding Cataract* (1936) with no greater success. After a promising start his writing career had got bogged down in a backwater.

The reason was not hard to see. From associating with Edwards, Collis had become a would-be intellectual. Ideas obsessed him. He proclaimed himself a lover of nature but he spent most of his time in the Reading Room at the British Museum. There he pored over the books that Edwards talked about – philosophers, metaphysicians, *The Golden Bough* – hoping to find satisfactory answers to the questions that bother students. In the process the museum became a kind of substitute church for him, the soft lights and hushed voices providing a pseudo-religious atmosphere which was very seductive. Whenever he could Collis always liked to get away to places where he knew he would not be found – the shed at the bottom of the garden, the side of a ship where he could gaze at the horizon undisturbed. The Museum was more of a cosy refuge than a place to discover the meaning of existence. There were times too when, even to Collis, it had the air of an asylum, frequented by men who, if he could have realised it at the time, were living witnesses to the folly and danger of looking for truth, or even trying to be a writer, in such a place:

At all times there are a number of foreign readers and theses-maddened Americans and a heterogeneous multitude who come in for various reasons: but one's picture and memory of the place is coloured by a vision of the habitués who were often eccentric. I think some readers were quite simply tramps who came in for warmth and shelter, tramps of a special kind who loved to be surrounded by books and to see people studying even if they don't do much reading themselves. I think of one man in particular. There is a swing-door entrance opening into a corridor leading to another swing-door into the Reading Room. In this corridor there used to be hot-water pipes. One of the readers took up a position there for a great deal of the time, gazing down at the pipes as if carefully examining them. He was quite broken down in person and dress. He was slight and small with almost no shoulders, and with decayed trousers creased concertina-fashion from thigh to foot. A long piece of string always dangled from the pocket of a miserable overcoat. He had so little face and so much battered hat that it was like a mouse wearing a hat. Occasionally he would sit in the Reading Room, but nearly always he would be found standing in the corridor carefully studying the pipes.

There were strange characters not always easy to make out. Once when having obtained a place at one of the crowded seats in the aisles between the main desks, I sat opposite a man who was writing very fast in an exercise book. He was not copying anything, but wrote very fast in his book, paused for a second or so, and then pushed forward again. I had seen him before rather vaguely and had noticed a certain abstracted air about him which did not seem congruous with composition. Now sitting opposite him I became amazed not only at his ceaseless writing but at his manner of writing which seemed to be sheer *scribbling*. I got up and walked about a little and finally stood behind him. I knew that he was unaware of me and that it would be safe to observe what he was writing. On he went, at a great pace, his pen racing across the paper, writing – *nothing*. It was just like this

ᒐᑎᑎᑎᑎᑎ ᒐᑎᑎᑎᑎ ᒐᑎᑎᑎᑎ ᒐᑎᑎᑎᑎ ᒐᑎᑎᑎᑎ

line after line with almost no variation, no letters formed. When he came to the end of his page he turned over and feverishly started on the next. I think he had been doing this for some time; he is doing it still, for I had another look only the other day, and there he was in a kind of enchantment, still bent on this strange task.

Collis did not pause to consider the strong symbolism of the poor mad scribbler. How narrow a gap separated him from the other apparently sane people, including Collis, in that Reading Room; how, for all the mark that they would make, those others might just as profitably have spent their days scribbling away as he did.

IV

Collis was a rare example of a man, the course of whose life was altered by a single unexpected decision – one which at the time would not have seemed to him, or anyone else, especially significant. Thanks to his determination to go his own way and not to compromise as far as his writing was concerned, his situation in the years before the war was truly desperate. His books did not sell, and the only recognition he had came from A. R. Orage, then editor of the *New English Weekly*, who regularly published his pieces. Looking back he found that time painful to recall. 'No words can describe the awfulness in terms of money anxiety,' he wrote. 'The financial problem was so appalling and so humiliating that I could not even look at the flowers in spring so much did bills come between me and them.' On 4 June 1931 he wrote in his notebook: 'Certainly it would seem no day could mark for me a lower depth. Utterly unwanted by the whole world as regards work . . . utter failure to make the best of the time I have got.'

In spite of his setbacks Collis refused to abandon his calling. He was convinced all his life that one day he would be recognised. This was not just some absurd piece of wishful thinking on his part. It was an inner conviction with perhaps a touch of second sight, which many Irish people have. This prophetic streak is borne out by a curious entry in his notebook in February 1931:

At the age of 30 and 31 I constantly think how delightful it will be to be a *vigorous* old man. I wait impatiently for old age. For how marvellous it will be to walk down the street unburdened by the problem of money, the problem of sex, the problem of housing, the problem of the literary battle; all these, including the problem of marriage, will have worked themselves out into solutions . . .

It is unusual, almost unknown, for a man of thirty to think about being old. But what logical reason could Collis have, any more than any other young man, for believing that old age would somehow bring an end to all his problems? Why should he think that just because he was old he would have no need to worry about money? Had he reflected for a moment, he would have realised that the opposite could be true and that the old, apart from all their other difficulties, are often desperately hard up. As a general view of old age there is no logic in it at all. Yet read as a private prophecy of what would happen to Collis himself, it is extraordinarily accurate. He *did* become a vigorous old man; he *was* happily married and comfortably housed; he *was* able to walk down the street without having to worry about his material problems. They had all worked themselves out into solutions.

In the meantime, however, his situation was bleak. At the beginning of 1932 he wrote

Must I descend still further into Hell? Things cannot go on worse, one thinks, and then they do get worse. For weeks and months now I have felt myself in the strangest way to be under Sentence of Time. Not until the Law permits it can things go right. Thus and thus and not otherwise is my doom. It is an extraordinary feeling this – that my hour is not yet, but that my hour will come. How horrible, how ghastly the middle period! What hell for those in any way dependent on me!

It was, if not Hell, at least a form of purgatory. If Collis had remained single, he might have endured it with greater success: for it is one thing for a man to have an immutable faith in his own destiny or genius or whatever he chooses to call it, and quite another for his wife to share that faith and put up with all the sacrifices it entails. What to him may seem courage and integrity, to her is likely to look like selfishness, bigotry and delusion. Eirene Collis was twenty-seven at the time of her marriage, and had known Collis for only a week. She was one of four daughters of Charles Holmes Joy MD of Tamworth in Staffordshire, and had trained in Oswestry and later at the Westminster Hospital as a physiotherapist, going on to practise privately in Hampstead. She was very pretty – small but delicate, alert, practical and fiercely ambitious both for herself and for her family. She didn't have much time for her sisters because, in her eyes, they achieved little in life. But her brother, who became a Commander in the Royal Navy, won her respect. She married Collis partly because she was convinced, like his friend Stephen Potter, that he was an exceptional man and she thought he was 'going places'. But as the years passed and Collis failed to follow up the sucess of his *Shaw*, she, not surprisingly, began to lose heart. Since 1932 Collis had been living near Sevenoaks in a cottage his father bought for him while Eirene, training to be a physiotherapist, remained in London with their two small daughters, Elizabeth and Gabrielle. It was not an ideal arrangement for a young family. In addition to her money worries, Eirene Collis had to cope with continuing ill health which in the days before the National Health Service meant doctors' bills and therefore more money worries. By the time war finally came the marriage was under severe strain. Eirene began to harry Collis, accusing him of burying himself in a 'funk hole' in the country. 'Why in God's name go and play mole in a country cottage for more than seven years?' she asked. Why didn't he write plays, or even get a job?

Goaded into anger by these familiar taunts, Collis replied to her in a handful of letters that laid bare all the tensions of their marriage, tensions which were to continue until Eirene's death:

You are incapable of making a helpful remark to me about my work, have never done so: any more than you have ever made an objective political remark, and unwound yourself from yourself . . .

Haven't you any sense, any tact? Don't you know that every year over two thousand couples separate because they find themselves incompatible? Don't you know we are? I stick by you because you are ill and have no one really but me, and I stick to you because always I remember the darling, darling, darling, darling, darling little Eirene, a simple pet completely at sea as to everything. How long am I going to hold on to that thread do you suppose?

What makes me savage and utterly despairing – that you don't *believe in me*, only vaguely in my 'gifts'.

And I know that you will never be happy with me except when I have plenty of money – that's the awful fact I have to face . . .

I am going to keep my integrity and go on and on and on – and I intend to make plays one of the attempts. And what is my wife's contribution in helping me with a battle far stiffer than at any time in English literary history? First, to be ill poor darling, you may not believe it, but when I think of what you suffer my eyes always fill with tears, and I know that, married to someone else, you would never have got so bad or perhaps ill at all. Second when we are in a war making an utter chaos of everyone's career and there is nothing left for it but the army as soon as possible, when a hundred bills overwhelm me, when 'getting a job' in London is like catching the moon, you write and say Change your establishment, get out of your funk hole.

My God!

It was now, in 1940, at the lowest point in the lives of the Collises, that their fortunes changed dramatically. Eirene received an offer out of the blue from the parents of an American girlfriend of Collis to go with her children to the States. In the meantime Collis had become gripped by a strange but powerful determination to become a farm labourer.

When I asked him about this turning point in his life, he used to say simply that with the coming of the war he 'had an opportunity to go on the land'. This was a mis-statement. He had no such opportunity. He forced himself onto the land against the wishes of several farmers. And before that he had made several attempts to get other forms of employment. He applied to Vickers Armstrong, the engineering firm. He went to see his Oxford friend Malcolm Macdonald at the Colonial Office to see if he could get into the army, but was told that his age group – he was now forty – was not yet eligible for call-up. Then the War Minister, Hore-Belisha, made a speech which seemed to suggest that older men might indeed be required for an emergency reserve of officers. Thinking that if he got into the army he would be given a desk job, he decided to become a farm labourer, come what may. Once he had made up his mind it became an obsession. As with his sudden decision to get married there was no special logic in his behaviour at this point. He had never before felt any urge to do manual labour, nor did he connect the move with his long-held feeling that 'his day would come'. He does not seem even to have related his

69

decision to his writing: he certainly did not think 'I will go and work on a farm and write a book about it.' He was simply gripped by an iron determination to work on a farm. In April 1940 he applied to a farmer called Maynard at Stonegate in Sussex, and was accepted for general work. Then on the Monday on which he was due to report for work, he received a letter telling him that he was no longer wanted. Collis decided, all the same, that he would go, and as he paced up and down Sevenoaks station on a cold April morning waiting for the Stonegate train he had a premonition that he would remember this particular moment for the rest of his life.

He went to the farm, agreed to work on a temporary basis for £1 a week, and was taken on. There was only one difficulty. He had let his Sevenoaks home and had nowhere to live near the farm. For a time he lodged with a friend but it meant a thirty-five-minute bicycle ride to and from work, which he found arduous, especially in the evenings. Then, one wet day, Collis was sent to break up potash at an old abandoned house near to the farm:

I carried on alone throughout the day at this, in the large old empty house. Enormous beams, many doors, three stairways, attics, cellars – the whole empty save for the sacks of artificial, some broken chairs, one wash basin, tools and potatoes, and in an upper room an enormous bedstead fitted with a mattress.

At lunchtime – or, more properly, dinner time – I went into this upper room. The bed certainly was formidable – one of those old Victorian 'beds like battlefields', as George Moore described them. There I had my meal, using the mattress as a table and chair. The house was tucked away in a lost corner, far from any other houses, with no road or even pathway to it. A lonely mansion at the best of times; on that day, that desolate room, one window stuffed up, one broken, one filled with cardboard, the wind whistling, the rain without and the damp within, I felt discouraged and inclined towards melancholy. I lay down on the bed, using my haversack as pillow, and, curling up, placed my overcoat over my body and head. The wind rattled the panes and various doors banged, but I felt secure now and remote from the world, as if I had buried myself.

Collis now asked Mr Maynard if he could live in the old house and he agreed. He moved his few pieces of furniture from Sevenoaks into two rooms. The one upstairs was a huge beamed bedroom with a fireplace large enough to accommodate a child's bed and long latticed windows with a view onto an oast house, which caught the evening sunlight: 'It was an ideal room, and all the time I was there I thought how I would hate to leave it when the time came.'

By now the war had begun in earnest:

The first bomb. It, or rather a number, came down on the neighbouring village. The explosion was so terrific that the ground shook the house, which still seems to me remarkable. It hurled me out of sleep. This being the first onslaught I had experienced, the impression was – The Invasion, the Conquest, the End. Simply because it seemed inconceivable that anything could stop or stay such violence – the violence seeming gigantic because of the noise. Looking from the window, seventeen moving poles of light pierced and prodded the sky and clouds, above which I could hear the German aeroplane. Oh the courage, the daring of the lone enemy up there – was my next feeling. Then the buzzing died away. The lights went out. I went back to bed. The Invasion, the Conquest, the End was over.

One of the most noticeable qualities of Collis's two wartime books, *While Following the Plough* and *Down to Earth*, is the air of great happiness and good humour that pervades them. For the first and almost the only time in his life he was carefree, at peace with himself and nature; and, in spite of the backbreaking nature of his work he was engaged in, felt fulfilled and inspired:

Often, then, my day now started with getting a horse harnessed into a cart and then jogging across the farm to load up something. The morning young, the sun slanting, mist clinging to the ground, the bird in the tree, hope in the heart – the eternal million-times repeated promise of the dawn. I was not making a living at all well by jogging along here, but I could not help feeling Alive, the freedom of the fields, the freedom of the sky, the freedom of movement gratuitously bestowed upon me – far more substantial than if I had been given the freedom of the City of Birmingham or had pressed into my hands huge Atlantic Charters and other paper monuments to the perfidy of Man.

The Vision of Glory was the title Collis gave to a later anthology of his writings on scientific phenomena. But it would have been better suited to his farming books. They are full of the exhilaration of a man whose eyes have been opened, a man who has passed through a gateway into another world. Until 1940 Collis still bore the marks of someone who has spent too much time in the British Museum Reading Room, whose ideas about nature were derived, in part, from books by fellow-writers. Now he found himself out in the open, face-to-face with the rough reality. Collis was genuinely amazed by what he discovered – the way in which crops grew and multiplied, the interaction of the elements, the power of the worm, the romance of the potato. He was as excited by it all as a small child who has been let into a nursery full of wonderful toys.

In all that he wrote there is no trace of the strain of war, or of the isolation that many men in his situation, cut off from family and friends, would have experienced. There were times when, working hard by himself in a field, he felt the depression familiar to all farm labourers. But the life, as a whole, suited his temperament. I am reminded of something Ruth Pitter said when I asked her how she thought Collis coped with the obscurity in which the greater part of his life was lived. 'Well,' she said, 'it's no worse than being a Holy Hermit.' Collis was not really a holy man, but there was something of the hermit in his nature and he spent many long periods on his own. He had no interest whatever in possessions or physical comfort. All through the war he lived in a variety of primitive farm houses and cottages with only his dog Bindo for company, but there is nothing to suggest that he ever felt lonely or deprived, or that he particularly missed his family, or craved the companionship of a woman. In his unpublished novel, *Progress of an Artist*, he described himself in the third person: 'Though an affectionate man and fond of society' – and, he might have added, of women – 'he was unafraid of loneliness. It was with surprise that he found himself exceptional in this . . . Nothing was more pleasant to him than to spend today, tomorrow and the next day without speaking to anyone . . .'

Collis had another asset, as far as working on a farm was concerned. He was physically very strong, and never suffered from any serious illness. In the same novel he wrote: 'He took great pride in the strength of his constitution and the beauty of

73

his limbs – which he had received from his father, who had been considered bodily almost a superman not made of flesh and blood or steel but of some rubbery substance equally proof against inward bacteria and objective violence.' Although he found the job exhausting he was able to work as hard as the 'professional' labourers who, probably for that reason, treated him with a respect – he was referred to throughout as 'Mr Collis' – that they would not have accorded to other part-time recruits from the cities. 'It is natural,' he wrote, 'for the countryman to enjoy seeing the townsman find the work too much.'

Health and strength were assets, but Collis could never live down the fact that he was not in any sense a practical man. Mechanical tasks were quite beyond him, and all his life he was accident-prone. Michael Holroyd remembers watching Collis from an upstairs window as he approached his house, seeing a dog lying in his path on the pavement and thinking that Collis, being Collis, would be bound to trip over the dog. He did. Alan Betts, his friend and neighbour in Ewell, remembers how, when organising a small party in his house, he laid in a bottle of gin but only one of tonic water; and how, another time, when he accidentally cut the telephone wire while he was clearing some ivy off his house he at once went inside to ring up the exchange and report the damage.

Before he became a farm worker Collis seems to have been quite unaware of his unworldliness. He was startled to be told one day by a land-girl on Maynard's farm, 'You're so absent-minded, they say.'

I was surprised at this. The last thing I had ever allowed myself to acknowledge was anything in the nature of the 'absent-minded professor'. Later I faced the matter and thought it out. Evidently I had been the subject of laughing commentary at the tea-table. Was it true after all? Come to think of it it was true! In ordinary life I had always forgotten things and mislaid them to an astonishing extent. Carelessness shows up badly on a farm. I used to drop things. I would load so many sacks on the cart, and on arriving at the other end would find that two had simply dropped off. Looking round for them I would see, a long way off, a lump on the track! Or I would hang a coat on the hames, and again, at journey's end, would miss it. I had forgotten all about it and had quite failed to realise that nothing stands jerking about unless it is tightly tied on. But the worst instance of forgetting things was one day, after the midday meal, I went right across to a field which I had to harrow, *without my horse*. This was recounted to me by the girl, who added that when I realised that I hadn't got the horse, I was seen running back madly. Now, no agricultural labourer is ever seen to run – except after rabbits at harvest. The spectacle of me (a) minus the horse and (b) running back to get it, had provided a sufficiently comic picture to raise a considerable degree of mirth.

In 1940 there was an acute shortage of petrol, and horses were again widely used for farm work. But Collis found it very difficult to handle a horse:

I hadn't realised that so 'simple' a matter as harnessing a horse and putting it in a cart entailed so many moves. I found that the same held true regarding what must seem to the man on the road to be the elementary performance of going through a gate. Yet it is quite remarkably more easy to gate-crash than to make a smooth passage. The thing must be done skilfully if you don't want to knock into one of the posts. On the whole I wasn't too much of a post-knocker, but this was due to the absence of many gates. There was something else much more difficult than a gate. The track from the house-end of the farm went down an incline and up another. At the bottom was a stream with

75

a bridge over it. The bridge was narrow, breaking down and with huge ruts near the edges. When it rained the mud was very thick on this clayey soil, and going over the bridge with a heavy load was extremely precarious. One wheel always fell into the rut at the very edge of the fenceless bridge, and in pulling the cart across the horse would generally lurch and slip. This bridge was in direct view of the house and the boss often watched this part of my journey with some anxiety – lest we fall over and the horse be injured, he explained.

Collis soon realised that the picture of the farm labourer which the public gets is quite false. The sight of people working in a field is peaceful, but for the workers themselves it is anything but. Even Thomas Hardy could get it wrong:

> Only a man harrowing clods
> In a slow silent walk
> With an old horse that stumbles and nods
> Half asleep as they stalk . . .

I find it difficult ever to say anything against Hardy (except with regard to *Tess*) but though the message of the poem perhaps requires that 'only', there seems to me now no excuse for the 'half asleep'. From the road a number of agricultural jobs look remarkably quiet, serene, slow, and easy: but if you stand beside the man in question you may find that he is putting out all his strength, is moving quite fast, and is in anything but a serene state of mind. I didn't find anything sleepy or serene about it. Not only is it impossible to walk with ease behind the harrow, since you are stumbling the whole time over the clods, but you can't *see* your work properly. You try to go straight across the field exactly beside your previous line, but you cannot see it without close inspection, and even when you do see it the horse is always standing you away from it, and in checking this you come back too much. Consequently you have the uncomfortable feeling most of the time that either you are going over ground already done or are missing out considerable areas. In short it is exasperating. Certainly not something you can do half asleep.

The Sussex farm was a small one of about a hundred acres, more than half of which was given over to apple orchards. The boss had built them up from scratch and had battled through many lean years. 'The struggle had left its mark on him,' Collis wrote. 'Melancholy by nature, he was now, I think, inclined to detest the world. I did not hear him say anything good of it or anyone in it.' In his memoirs Collis tells us that Maynard offended him on a number of occasions, 'and one in particular', unspecified. He got on better with the foreman Morgan – 'about thirty, non-rustic in appearance, quiet, accentless, pleasant and exceedingly grave'. Morgan was fond of reading and Collis lent him Hardy and even *War and Peace* – 'but he did not enjoy it.' His other fellow worker he called Arthur Miles – though I assume that this was not his real name, as Collis was much less kind about him:

Arthur Miles was a rough diamond. At many farms, it seems, there is one man who is 'always right', who 'knows everything' who puts everyone right and shouts loudly. An ordinary man might say 'You will find it in the shed' or 'You've got it the wrong way round', without undue emphasis or excitement. Arthur would yell the information in apparent fury. He was a tremendous blusterer. But an efficient blusterer, the regular handy man always called upon in difficulties for masterly improvisation.

In 1947 Collis was regrettably unable to spell out Arthur's favourite word which was 'bugger' – a word which Collis said had long lost its etymological significance:

77

Swearing came as naturally to Arthur as leaves to a tree, and having command over all the possible variations in which the word could be used it came from his lips, almost in terms of a song – 'It's a bugger', 'well I'm buggered', 'he's a bugger', 'you can bugger off'. Once when I heard him preserve silence for a few minutes on account of the proximity of the boss's wife, it seemed unnatural and disquieting, and I felt anxious for him until he started up again.

Neither Arthur nor his wife, who worked alongside Collis, took especially to their new recruit. 'How do you like this *wurk*, Mr Collis,' she would shout when they were threshing 'this is *wurk*.' Once when they were packing up apples together Collis who was feeling full of beans, said to her jokingly, 'Mrs Miles, would you see that they fill up the sacks properly?' She flew into a rage, screaming 'I don't take no orders from nobody. I'm not taking no orders from you, I only take orders from the boss.' Collis thought it best to say nothing, but Mrs Miles kept on railing against him for the whole of that afternoon and would not allow him to forget his remark. A few days later, when he was doing some hedging, he heard her talking in a loud voice to some visitors. 'Who is that?' one of them asked. '*Oh that's nobody. He's only a workman here,*' she said.

Light relief was provided by the presence of land-girls, drafted into farmwork for the duration of the war. Maynard also employed girls from university who, because they were not afraid of being sacked, treated their work in a more frivolous spirit than the full-timers. Once on a hot day some of the girls stripped off and went swimming in one of the many ponds on the farm. Morgan was furious when he spotted them and debated whether he should remove their clothes, eventually deciding against it, to the great disappointment of Collis and the rest.

The other diversion during that historic summer of 1940 was the Battle of Britain, fought in the skies over Kent and watched by Collis and the farm workers. On 16 September a major battle took place overhead, heralded by a siren at eight o'clock in the morning. As the Spitfires joined battle against the German invaders bullets began to fall and Collis crawled under a cart for safety. Afterwards a collection was taken and a notice posted up in the village.

STONEGATE ENTERTAINMENT TAX
£3. 15. 3d.
COLLECTED FOR SPITFIRE FUND
FROM ONLOOKERS OF THE SCRAP.
SEPTEMBER 16 1940.

Maynard's farm was mainly devoted to fruit growing, and the work force was therefore seasonal. After a few months Collis was laid off and had to look elsewhere. In the Spring of 1941 he was offered a job by a Dorset farmer, Rolf Gardiner at Fontmell Magna. Yet, once again, at the last minute, with his possessions already loaded into a van, Collis was told, by telegram, that he was not after all required; and once again he decided to ignore the telegram and go to Dorset.

He arrived and was by no means made welcome. 'The subsequent hours,' he said, 'were among the very lowest of my life, the most miserable.' But as before, his determination simply to ignore the wishes of others paid off. He was befriended by some neighbouring farmers and eventually got a part-time job working for a small farmer called Mr Law at Tarrant Gunville, who also supplied him with a bungalow. Later he found he was able, after all, to work for Rolf Gardiner doing forestry work, work that he described in the second of his two farming books, *Down to Earth*.

Collis was now seized by a determination to become a ploughman. He enjoyed forestry work but he hankered after a mixed farm where he would be able to use a plough. He learned that there was a job going at Fordingbridge in Hampshire, but for the third time in succession was told at the eleventh hour not to come. Before he could repeat his procedure of turning up regardless, he heard that a farmer at Tarrant Gunville, a Mr Hannan, was short of labour. He went to see him at once, and told him that he was 'quick on the uptake' with regard to farming matters – something of a mis-statement, as he himself was prepared to admit. He was given the job.

If Hannan had known that Collis was to immortalise him, warts and all, he might have thought twice about taking him on. It was an irony that Collis, who in later years liked to think of himself primarily as a 'prose poet', a man who had successfully explained scientific phenomena in language that ordinary people could understand, should be best known for his portrait of Hannan, a figure whom anyone acquainted with the land immediately recognised as the archetypal farmer, memorably described in the book by a single capital letter and an apostrophe as 'E:

He was sometimes called the boss, and sometimes merely 'the Van'. He used a second-hand butcher's van for getting about the premises and carrying oil and what not from one scene of operation to another. So we would hear – 'Look out, there's the Van!' or 'I didn't see no Van' when his whereabouts was doubtful. But on the whole he was designated simply as 'E – ''E's coming!' It was as 'E that I think of him and as 'E that I shall refer to him.

He was a man somewhere in the fifties. His eyes were impressive in their mildness, but his mouth was large and ugly, partly concealed by a stumpy moustache. You could recognise him a long way off by his walk. He took huge strides, head bent slightly down, like a man measuring a cricket pitch. That walk was very characteristic. There was no dawdling nor diddling about with him: he never strolled: he never looked round quietly at the scene: he never took out a pipe, nor smoked a cigarette, any more than he would be likely to drink a glass of beer, pat a dog, or say good night, good morning, or thank you.

Having adopted a certain pace – a terrific pace – he meant to keep it up. He neither would nor could slow down a bit. ''E'll break up one of these days,' they would say at intervals. He did not intend to lose a minute if he could help it – for time was money to him as certainly as to any business man. An atmosphere of hurry and almost of crisis prevailed whenever he was around, for he was his own foreman. He was also one of his own labourers, so to speak, for he joined in anything and everything, no job was beneath him. In this way he got a tremendous amount of work out of his men as he set the pace, and each person felt that he had his eye on him – and he had.

Like the other labourers, Collis was caught up in the constant tension which 'E generated. He became nervous, finding it difficult to follow and then to remember the instructions he was given. One morning 'E would say to him – 'Take the cultivator back to the centre field, then drag the field you cultivated yesterday. The drags are in the field next to the house. Put one each on they ones that have slides, then take 'ee up to the field. You'll find a 'ole by the straw rick in the beanfield. When you've finished there get the roller and do the wheat field.' His job was made more difficult by the feeling that whatever attempts he made to carry out such instructions, he would be watched by 'the Van'. A few days later when he was harrowing a field, 'E appeared from nowhere and ticked him off for getting water for his tractor from the farm house – 'Waste of juice, going right over there when there is a trough in the field. Use your brains!' Collis could not see the point of this. For even if he took his tractor to the trough he had nothing to use as a filter. It was a sign of his magnanimity and his detachment that he was not a bit offended by 'E's abruptness. Thinking it over afterwards he concluded: 'I am not a brainy man in any marked degree, though my capacity to use what brains I possess and to pick the brains of others is second to none.' What 'E meant, he decided, was that he lacked not brains but ingenuity and the ability to improvise that a farm worker needs to cope with all the little unforeseen mishaps of the average day. He decided in future to cultivate ingenuity and the next time his tractor needed water took it to the trough and used his hat as a filter.

There were six full-time workers on the farm in addition to Collis. The youngest was called Dick, the senior was Robert the shepherd, an old man with a very loud voice who resented the presence on the farm of Collis's dog Bindo because it was always scrapping with his sheep-dog:

In his youth he must have been uncommonly handsome. He was still very good-looking, strikingly so; completely rustic, his features, nose, cheek-bones, set of eyes were yet at the same time aristocratically fine shaped. Nor was this a passing fancy of mine: it struck me later whenever I caught him in profile on a rick. His eyes also, a pale

washed blue, were beautiful, except when they flared up in some out-
burst.

Once, when they were all working together building a hayrick,
Robert shouted at Collis, 'Before the war you wouldn't be on
this rick, an if you'd seen I and t'others working here, you'd have
thought us a lot of mugs I allow' – adding 'I think after the war
we should change jobs and I'll take my ease.'

'I'd like to see you take on my job which seems so easy,' Collis
replied, thinking that he had successfully concealed from the
others that he was a writer, 'but you don't know what it is.'

'Yes I do,' Robert shouted, 'it's a p——'

'What's that?' Collis asked, not able to make out what he had
said.

'A poit, a writer,' Robert yelled. 'I could go out into that field
and write a hundred pages as good as any, but I wouldn't do it.
It's too easy. I wouldn't do it. If I did do it, at the end of the day
my fingers would *tingle with shame*.'

Dick was only twenty and took no pleasure in his work. For
that reason he never once sought to be one up on Collis, to get a
rise out of him or put him right. Dick came nearest to becoming
a friend. He would have liked to see the world, and wanted to
study. Collis lent him H. G. Wells's *Outline of History*, which he
read twice. But handing over the large book presented problems, as neither wanted to be seen by the others. Collis arranged
to pass it on to Dick surreptitiously behind a hedge when they
finished work. But just at that moment Robert passed. 'You've
got sommat there to get on with, I allow,' he said in a low voice
and hurried on.

Harold, normally the tractor driver, had lived in the village all his life and had no desire to travel. He told Collis he never read anything. Alf was, like Collis, a newcomer from the town trying his hand at farm work. He was a nervous little man, more apprehensive than anyone at the approach of 'E and didn't stay long on the farm, telling Collis, when he left, that he was the only person who had addressed him in a friendly way and who had bothered to find out his Christian name.

'Even when a man leaves,' Collis noted, 'he seldom bothers to say goodbye to his mates – he just packs up and disappears. He discovered that, again, contrary to popular conceptions of farming life, there was little camaraderie among the workers. They kept their distance not only from him but from one another. Collis, with his self-sufficient nature, was quite happy with this arrangement, which suited him very well. As it was, the only thing that constituted a bond between them was common antipathy towards 'E and a shared desire to outwit the Van whenever possible. Collis describes a typical occasion when he was hoeing with Harold and Dick:

We were working now on a field along which the main track ran. Hence the approach of the van was easily seen. When it was discerned approaching, our pace would quicken: not too fast, since that would look bad, too obvious; but appreciably, while we asked 'Is 'E going to stop?' If the van stopped then we might expect 'E to alight and come across, look on, make a criticism, and possibly join us. This was always a critical moment when the Van was seen – Will 'E stop, join, and spoil the morning? became the great question. One occasion was rather amusing. Harold, Dick and myself were going along our rows side by side across the field, our cut reached to about the middle of the field, when normally we would turn about. We were working towards the track when the Van appeared coming up, and then stopped. 'E got out and went over into the next field to talk to Robert, and there remained for some time. We couldn't see him, but had to suppose that he could see us. At last he appeared again. Would he now come over to us? But no, he got into the van. But it didn't start off at once; evidently he was watching us. We were still working towards the track, towards him. We came to the end of our cut. We should now have stopped, picked up our new rows and gone back. But Harold said 'Keep on, don't stop, keep on: if 'e sees us stop 'e'll come over, sure thing. Keep on and 'e'll bugger off!' And though we had come to the end of our cut we kept going now on ground which we had already hoed ('E wouldn't be able to notice this at the distance), and continued keeping on until the crisis passed and 'E got back into the van and did at last bugger off.

Collis worked at Hannan's farm throughout the war, and by the end of that time was a reasonably efficient, as well as hard-working, labourer. He could build a rick, take a horse and cart through a gate without demolishing the gate-post, knew how to clean the sparking plugs on the tractor and had altogether lost his nervousness in the presence of 'E. For his part, 'E had so much confidence in Collis that he was prepared to entrust him with ploughing a field – the one job he had hankered after when he first came to the farm. Working with a tractor, Collis performed the job so well that when 'E inspected his work he said 'That's good enough for I.' Collis did his best not to look too surprised and pleased. Later, on another farm, he was given a chance by a Norwegian-born farmer, Sigvart Godeseth, to plough with a horse, describing the subsequent four months as the happiest time of his life:

'If I were asked the straight question,' he wrote,

whether I would prefer to plough, *always* with horse or tractor, I might find it difficult to answer, since I very much enjoy working with a tractor and a three-furrow plough –

Yet nothing can compare with the simple, strenuous horse-work. For one thing there is no other physical work to compare with it: there is not a game in the world that can make you feel half so good. And, fascinating as the machine work is, you do not hold the plough. But it is just this *grasping* of the handles of the plough, both arms stretched out fully and often putting out full strength, that somehow is the very top notch of satisfaction. Ah, I say, even as I write these lines, give me the plough handles that I may grip them and strike out across the field! release me from this chair! (for it is much easier to do a thing than write about it, so much easier to perform than reveal). And to be able to see your work directly in front of you all the time, to watch your wave rise and fall to silence in your wake – this you cannot get the other way. But again I say, it is the grasping of the handles for which there is no substitute, no compensation. Then your feet are upon the earth, your hands are upon the plough. You seem to be holding more than the plough, and treading across more than this one field: you are holding together the life of mankind, you are walking through the fields of time . . .

V

While Following the Plough, the little book that Collis wrote about his life as a farm labourer, was his masterpiece. Unlike much of his writing, which was often overworked and over-polished, this book has an immediacy and freshness which derived from the fact that he had, throughout his farming years, kept a diary and written down his experiences at the end of each day. Re-reading the book in 1980 for the first time since its publication he wrote to Martyn Skinner,

I have been surprised at the variety of things I have worked into it. When all is said and done, I suppose, this is a really 'creative' book, a world of people and nature captured and mirrored – my only book that is a whole in that way, an experienced whole. Thank goodness I had the guts to keep a diary at that time, no matter how exhausted. It is amazing how the recorded remarks, for instance, made by the people give life to it all . . .

Written in short sections, each with its own heading, the book is a series of scenes and essays in which Collis skilfully alternates between his autobiography and more philosophical reflections on life in general. This format suited him very well. He never really mastered the long narrative but excelled at the short piece – occasionally breaking off, as he said, to 'raise it up' with a purple passage, which could be all the more effective coming on the heels of a down-to-earth scene of farm life involving 'E and his small band of workers.

As often seems to happen with masterpieces, Collis found it very hard to get his book accepted by any publisher. All his life he had trouble placing his books, becoming resigned to the polite letters of rejection: 'We have read your manuscript with great interest . . . fascinating account . . . vivid detail . . . regret to have to inform you . . . not sufficient market for this type of book . . . best wishes . . .' In the case of *While Following the Plough* no less than twelve publishers turned the book down before Jonathan Cape, who had published his book on Shaw in 1925, finally accepted it, though even then with a rather ill grace.

It was an attractive, readable account, Cape himself wrote to Collis, but it was not really good enough: 'The book wants going over and pointing up – it is not up to your standard. I think if you go over it you will find a good deal of revision is necessary.'

Attached was a distinctly tepid and schoolmasterly memorandum from Cape's reader, Daniel George:

It is not hard to put one's finger on typical examples of the slack writing in this ms. On page two 'the serried ranks of apple trees' is a frightful cliché and quite inexact at that. In the fourth line from the bottom of this page there is a grammatical solecism which is repeated throughout the book, 'I would like to have got'. After past conditionals the present infinitive, not the perfect infinitive, is the correct form. The phrase should read '"should (not would) have liked to get . . .' I notice on page 5 'Owing to my very early breakfast . . . I began to wonder how on earth . . .' I don't call this writing. Too many sentences throughout the ms. begin with 'Owing to . . .' Some of the author's philosophical reflections and obiter dicta seem to me scarcely worth recording and his humour is weak . . . The plain truth is that the book has not yet been *written*. The material is exellent, the author is an interesting person, the subject can never grow stale; but there is a growing reader-resistance to 'agricultural' books and only a really first-rate one can now get by. *Following the Plough* is not quite good enough in its present state, but if the author really worked on it he could make an excellent book of it.

Collis was especially proud of his response to this critique, which he instanced as an example of his Irish *shrewdness* when it came to dealing with people like publishers. After a suitable interval he returned the manuscript saying that having taken advantage of their kind criticisms, he had made substantial amendments. In fact he had done nothing – though he did correct some of the solecisms that George had detailed. Cape's however expressed themselves 'delighted with the improvements' and duly published the book in July 1946.

Like all of Collis's books it had generally favourable treatment from reviewers. The only exception was John Moore, author of the Brensham Trilogy and himself well known as a writer on country life. Moore complained that the book was 'arid' and that Collis was too self-absorbed. 'He is mainly interested,' he wrote, 'if not in himself, at any rate in his own mind . . . and though from time to time other characters intrude upon the scene . . . they have no real existence, no life independent of the author.' It was a curious account of a book which contains so many vivid portraits of farm workers and especially of 'E. Collis for his part never forgave John Moore. 'Whenever his books came out,' he told me, 'I got hold of them and put the boot in.' Other critics, however, were more responsive. 'His book is not merely the record of what befell him. It is a record coloured by the attractive personality of the author,' Howard Spring wrote in *Country Life*. Middleton Murry called it an 'excellent book' which gave 'an extraordinarily accurate picture of the work and life of a big English arable farm'.

Most book reviews are written in a hurry by people who have no strong feelings either for or against. An author is lucky if *one* critic grasps the point of what he has tried to do. In Collis's case, the novelist and playwright Charles Morgan wrote a long two-column review in the *Sunday Times* notable for its profundity and perception. Collis, he said, had written a book of

extremely various interest. He says modestly that there 'is no instruction in it, and that his approach is one of 'genuine ignorance' but, for the very reason that he begins at the beginning and describes 'operations and implements as if the reader were as fresh to them' as he was himself, what he writes on matters of fact is alive and illuminating; it enables those of us who share his first ignorance to share his discovery, to see and feel and smell what he was about.

Morgan, alone of the critics, recognised the importance of what had happened to Collis as a writer:

Among the consequences of war's having become total war is the compulsion upon men and women to lead lives altogether different from their normal lives. This compulsion forces upon them a chance which is the effective theme of Mr Collis's book, to correct the distortions of their view – to see life afresh and to discover a harmony within it.

I am not now thinking of the fighting men, for at all times young civilians have been 'pressed' or have volunteered. What is new in our experience is the extent to which the non-fighting population – the men over-age, the women, and, even the children – are compelled when the war comes to a revolution in their lives. Everyone is not fully affected: everyone's life is not revolutionised: many continue in their own homes and their old tasks, working in changed and more difficult conditions: but many others cease altogether to be what they were and adopt a way of life, a total disguise, contrary to their previous idea of themselves.

This is what happened to Mr Collis when, having been all his life a man of letters, he became a farm-labourer: and the interest of his book lies not only – and, for me, not chiefly – in his account of the land, but in the evidence it gives that the compulsion to revolutionise one's life may also be an opportunity, while moving from one material method of existence into another, to be reborn.

'I am anxious to say a word about the potato.' This was the unusual opening sentence of *Down to Earth*, a sequel to *While Following the Plough*, written in the same arrangement of short pieces and published in the same format with wood engravings by David Koster. Collis had begun here to develop what he considered his *forte*, the examination of simple, taken-for-granted natural phenomena like the potato and the exposition of the complex and miraculous forces that he found at work, turning the dry findings of scientists into poetry and religious truth. There was no logical reason why he could not have done this work in his British Museum days. In practice, however he needed the personal involvement with the growing of potatoes in order to be able to write about them. He had to dig, to plant and harvest before he could write. Then there was no stopping him.

Collis was proud of the fact that he started from a position of unashamed ignorance. 'I always start from square one,' he told me, 'without knowing anything, because I never have known anything. My whole strength lies in my ignorance and stupidity.' But in this lay part of his appeal because, in his ignorance, he was really no different from anyone else.

91

I found when I had written it that no one else knew what a potato was. And it made quite a stir. A local schoolmaster gave a lecture on the potato to his school. A bishop preached a sermon on the potato in the church. A cabinet minister said that I had *saved* the potato. And all I did, you see, was simply to say what a potato is –

'When we eat a potato we eat the earth, and we eat the sky. It is the law of nature that all things are all things. That which does not appear to exist today is tomorrow hewn down and cast into the oven. Nature carries on by taking in her own washing. That is Nature's economy, contrary to political economy; so that he who cries "Wolf! Wolf!" is numbered amongst the infidels. "A mouse," said Walt Whitman "is enough to stagger sextillions of infidels." Or a potato. What is an infidel? One who lacks faith. What creates faith? A miracle. How then can there be a faithless man found in the world? Because many men have cut off the nervous communication between the eye and the brain. In the madness of blindness they are at the mercy of intellectual nay-sayers, theorists, theologians, and other enemies of God. But it doesn't matter; in spite of them, faith is reborn whenever anyone chooses to take a good look at anything – even a potato.'

'But I was equally good on the worm,' he went on with disarming self-esteem. The worm, like the potato, was a paradox. In fact the whole of Collis's message in so far as he had such a thing was to stress the paradoxical. In this he resembled G. K. Chesterton, a writer whom he admired very much. Both started from the premise that the natural world, which people ignore or take for granted, is miraculous. 'It is not the rabbit out of the hat but the rabbit out of the rabbit that is so extraordinary,' Collis once wrote in a sentence worthy of Chesterton. He followed it up by observing that not only was nothing quite what it seemed, but it was often the exact opposite: 'If you say what a thing is, it turns out to be either upside down or a paradox or extraordinary, because there is nothing more extra-ordinary than the ordinary in the world.' Eyeless, legless, face-less, earless, voiceless, the worm to the outward eye was the weakest, the most insignificant creature on the earth –

Some people know nothing of the worm save that it will turn under certain unspecified circumstances. Others when they have cut one in half, honestly feel that they have performed an act of creation, making two creatures proceed where there had been only one before. There are no songs in its name. True, the poet who bent the most concen-trated gaze upon the tiger, and saw that in it the fire of light burned brightest, was also he who, looking down into the damp, dark earth, perceived the worm and said – 'Art thou a worm? Image of weakness, art thou but a worm? I see thee like an infant wrappèd in the lily's leaf.' Yet even he may not have known that the worm is more powerful than the tiger, that by its vast operations in ploughing, in harrowing, in levelling, in draining, in airing, in manuring, and even in creating soil, it adds to the wealth of nations and governs the destiny of man; and that given time and condition it could remove a mountain and cause a city to vanish from the face of the earth.

Still, in writing this and other similar passages Collis was acting himself in a worm-like way, regurgitating the findings of others. He was quite happy to admit this, again referring to Chesterton: 'The business of the artist like G.K.C. is to extract what he can from specialists in the way of fact. Get your fact, drag it from its dull context. Only by reading heavy stuff can you break out into light; only by wading through oceans of dullness can you give flight to fancy.' Though he wrote a great deal about scientific matters, Collis was never a scientist and never thought of himself as one. In *Down to Earth* he admits very candidly that

93

'Experiments don't *work* for me.' Once he read in Cobbett's *The Woodlands* how, if you leave an ash seed in water for four days and then cut it open, 'you will see, standing as upright as a dart, an *ash* tree, with leaves, trunk and stem: that is to say the head of the root and all this you will see with the naked eye, as clearly as you ever saw an *ash* tree growing in a field or meadow.'

'Being exceedingly eager to see this,' Collis writes,

I tried the experiment carefully. But I did not see it. I often tried but I never saw the little tree. Using a razor blade I slit the casket that holds the kernel, according to instructions, and I did find something. I found a very neat miniature *spade*. It was exceedingly attractive and surprising to look at, but it was not a tree.

The same thing happened when he decided to try to verify by personal observation the findings of Darwin with regard to worms and their capacity to move earth, findings which he himself had used as the basis of his hymn of praise to the worm:

One day when strolling in a great Cathedral Cloister, I observed that the grass in the middle contained many flat-slabbed tombstones, some modern, some quite ancient. How interesting, I thought, here I shall be able to see the result of worm-burial before my eyes. I saw a modern stone, 1921, how it was level with the grass, and near it another stone, 1804, which had sunk a considerable distance below the surface. This was excellent. I walked round so that I might see the old tombstones well sunk while the newer ones were still on the surface. I came to Martha Hunt, of Beloved Memory, dated 1870, and then to Nathaniel Groves, Resting in the Lord, dated 1791. But Martha Hunt's tombstone had sunk lower than that of Nathaniel Groves! Trying not to notice this, I passed on and continued to conduct my researches. Some of the other stones conformed to the requirements of the theory but not all.

94

In neither case would Collis consider for a moment that Cobbett or Darwin might be wrong, the one in relation to the ash seed and the other to the earth worm. He felt that there must be something the matter with *him* which made it psychologically impossible for such experiments to turn out well for him. 'I fear,' he concluded, 'that I have nothing of the scientist in me, nothing of the naturalist or botanist: I shall never propose a theory supported by experimental proof, I shall never discover anything, never make new things known. I am content to make known things new.'

In the second half of *Down to Earth*, Collis describes his experiences as a forester working for Rolf Gardiner. Gardiner was an unusual farmer – an ecologist and conservationist at a time when such things were unheard of. He admired the writings of D. H. Lawrence, and strove to uphold the framework of the old rural way of life that was slipping away. One of his schemes was to re-claim and re-stock the ancient forest land of Cranborne Chase, and it was to help in this work that Collis was engaged. Describing his short career as a forester, Collis reverted to the style of *While Following the Plough*, with the result that the book came alive. He always saw himself as a teacher, a man who expounded scientific truths in a plain and poetic way. He shut his eyes to the idea that his writing might be much more vivid and effective when he wrote from personal experience, when he described his work, his own work, his own observations, rather than elaborating the findings of others.

The great difference now was that Collis was working on his own. But he didn't mind this. Nowhere does he complain about the lack of human company. Instead, when conditions were right, he seemed to attain a state of blissful happiness working in the wood. His job was to clear about twelve acres of woodland to leave enough space for chosen ash trees to grow. He worked with an axe and a billhook, putting his head down and slashing his way 'through the undergrowth, brushing up the clinging thorn, the entangling and infuriating privet and hacking down the honeysuckle's parasitic climbers'. He found the work satisfying because, as he said, there was so much to show for it: 'In quite a short time I had made a distinct impression, a definite clearing – the jumble of brambles and shrubs and misshapen trees had vanished from the space I had worked upon and now just a few straight ash trees stood up clear and free.'

During his time in the wood Collis developed a great affection for the ash tree: 'One of the reasons why I am especially attracted by ash is because it has so much fire in it,' he wrote.

That may not be the proper way to put it but it certainly seems as if flame resides inside the wood . . . and of all trees, Ash becomes fire best. It need not be seasoned first, it burns almost equally well whether dry or cut down yesterday. If you cut down a bundle of fresh, green ash twigs they do perfectly for lighting your fire, they are ready made crackers, they are children's fireworks. Try the same thing with hazel and you'll never get your fire lit at all.

Another advantage of the ash from Collis's point of view was that it was among the last of the trees to come into leaf in springtime. This meant one thing – more sunshine. All his life Collis was a sun-worshipper. If the sun was shining he had to sit or lie in it. And, like a small boy, he hated having to wear socks and shoes and took them off whenever he could. 'Sometimes I could wish,' he wrote, 'that my love of the sun were less genuine

. . . the sun deflects me from my courses.' Collis worked very hard as a woodman and in the springtime his ideal was to make himself so tired with his work that he could then lie down in the sun and go to sleep:

I chose some particular spot at the foot of an ash to which the sun came and at each side of which I had placed drifts. At the chosen moment I lay down, curled up, and closed my eyes while the sun shone on my face. Often a strong chilly wind blew, but it didn't come near me, I received only the sun. Then I entered my own special, simple paradise. I was absolutely tucked away from the world – several miles in all directions from it – I was totally hidden from sight of mortal soul, and no one knew where I was nor would be coming anywhere near me. I was free from the entire turmoil of the world. I lay there, almost sinking into, melting into the earth, waiting for sleep to come and take me right down – wondering if death in reality is more than such a joyous sinking down as this. But truly now I indulged in no thoughts, no metaphysical speculations, I became little higher than an animal – and no lower. I laughed to think what a reprehensible sight I would have made to any *busy* man who came upon me there, a sloping slacker, an untoiling son of the earth! But I felt no need to offer up apologies to the unreproving beings around. Let the world outside carry on, I would say, let them dash hither and thither, let them kill one another wholesale, let them go to hell, I'm wrapped in the embrace of Nature and filled with peace and love! And like any dog, like any savage, I lay there enjoying myself, harming no man, selling nothing, competing not at all, thinking no evil, smiled on by the sun, bent over by the trees, and softly folded in the arms of the earth.

At other times Collis became possessed by superhuman energy. He liked to work in the heat, stripping off his shirt:

Thus unencumbered I can do, and like doing, a week's work in two days. The hotter I get the harder I work, perspiration making me almost cold and the sun not hot enough to make me feel its heat then. The sheer freedom of the limbs with the breeze on the body gives a pleasure not easily excelled: one could justifiably enthuse about it: I content myself with saying that though this is not the only way of feeling happy and alive, it is one way. To use the mind at full concentration is one of the most manly things we can do, since this capacity happens to be the special gift of man: but we are also animals, and we experience great joy when in primitive surroundings we are not dolled up and tied down with artificial skins. Thus with me anyway. I cannot exaggerate the satisfaction I get from becoming a 'savage' . . .

In this state of exhilaration he sometimes worked on for hours at a stretch axing huge trees, cleaning them up and chopping them into poles short enough to load onto a lorry.

The only company that Collis had during his time as a forester was an old woodman, who occasionally came to the wood with his grandson to make hurdles out of the hazel that Collis had cut down. For the first and only time he met someone who conformed to the traditional idea of the 'old countryman' – a man well into his seventies, who had spent his whole life doing the same job and never hankering for change or travel or variety. This old man was likewise the only person who shared Collis's religious view of nature. Once Collis made a remark about the anti-religious trend of workers in the modern world:

It pleased him, for presently he came out with a generalisation of his own without any prompting from me. He glanced round the wood, and slowly and haltingly choosing his words said 'If I do say to a farmer now, Look how they plants do grow: look at thik field of yourn and see how they do grow without help; there must be a wonderful God behind they plants – he would not understand I.'

Collis had time now and leisure to observe the work of nature without fear of the unexpected arrival of the Van. There were deer in the wood and many smaller animals; and also wild flowers. 'It is quite obvious that the foxglove cannot be *improved*,' he wrote, 'there is no progressing beyond that point for that particular appearance. There is no room for improvement in the bluebell nor in any other of the exhibits.'

But as summer wore on, the trees thickened and the atmosphere became at times oppressive:

By June the more obvious flowers have completed their act, they have had *their* summer, their autumn and are now in their winter of desolation. We have become accustomed to the green of the trees. The birds are reticent. In July a hush falls upon everything. The silence is disquieting. The silence of a wood at all times is something to reckon with: it seems to pervade one's personality, and I seldom open my lips even to speak to my dog. In such an atmosphere ambition wilts, mental strife seems futile, the arts unreal. Filled with unease, one would gladly leave the silent and too solemn trees for a more human scene.

Collis was therefore pleased when his job was done. All the same, he looked back at his days in the wood as the most fulfilling time of his life:

Nothing I have ever done has given me more satisfaction than this, nor shall I ever hope to find again so great a happiness. Realising something of what the work meant to me and perhaps truthfully saying that he was very pleased with the result, Rolf entered this area of about twelve acres in the books of the estate as COLLIS PIECE, and by that name it is now known. Thus then do I achieve what had never occurred to me could conceivably happen, that a piece of English earth and forest would carry my name into the future. Nobody is ever likely to confer upon me Honours or Titles or City Freedoms, nor will any Monument be raised to perpetuate and repeat my name. But this plot of earth will do it, these trees will do it: in the summer they will glitter and shine for me and in the winter, mourn.

VI

Down to Earth was published in August 1947, again to very
favourable reviews. But the critics turned out to be more
interested in Collis's 'scientific' passages than his autobiography. 'Mr Collis uses scientific fact not as the scientists do but as
the raw material of the poet and the seer,' H. W. Massingham
wrote in *Time and Tide*. 'Nor is his philosophy abstracted from
reality in the modern way: he utters his wisdom as a ploughman
and a woodman. "We see into the life of things," as Wordsworth
wrote, and out of the wonder of what he has seen has come a
wonderful book.' The doyen of book reviewers, Desmond
MacCarthy, who had been introduced to Collis's writings by
Charles Morgan's earlier review of *While Following the Plough*,
was also enthusiastic about his insights into the natural world.
He noted that there were echoes in the book of Edward
Carpenter –

something too in the author's description of physical zest and mental
rest of Tolstoy's Levin sweating and toiling among the reapers. But the
prime characteristic – what arrested me at once – was something
different: this was the prominence in it given to scientific explanations
of natural processes, while the writer's attitude towards them remained poetical and religious.

As it turned out, this investigation of natural phenomena was
to preoccupy Collis for the rest of his life. The elucidation of
scientific facts in a 'poetical and religious' way became his main

vocation, though he combined it with biography. Once again, it might have turned out very differently. No reader of *Down to Earth* could miss the note of exhilaration sounded during his time as a forester and a farm worker, during which he was able to alternate strenuous physical work and writing. He thought, as he said, that he had discovered the ideal existence. With another writer this could be dismissed as sentimentalism, but not with Collis. He was physically capable of very hard work and he enjoyed it almost as much as playing tennis. His temperament was suited to the isolation, and his demands in terms of money and possessions were minimal. Why then, in 1947, did he give it all up and go and live in suburban Surrey?

As usual, at these crucial turning points, his autobiography fails to provide a satisfactory answer. All he says is this: 'After the war I would have remained on the land combining the security of farm work with my literary endeavours but I abandoned this idea so that we might all live together near Carshalton.' Once again I find that Collis is not even accurate as to facts. His daughter Elizabeth tells me that before moving to Carshalton, they lived first at a house at Glenilla Road, Hampstead. Here, she remembers, her father was miserable, especially when his dog Bindo, who had been with him throughout his farming years, was run over by a car.

That one inaccurate sentence remains all by way of explanation of Collis's return to urban life, the reader being left to make what he may of it. It is noticeable that he says he 'would have remained on the land', rather than 'could'. In other words, his preference was to stay in Dorset and carry on as a farm labourer. But he was forced to alter his course by what had happened to his wife Eirene during the war. As he explains, in 1940 she had gone in a state of poor health to America with their two small children. Shortly after her arrival she had an operation for hysterectomy, during which she nearly died. The operation may well have altered her personality, as it so often does, making her more forceful and masculine. Later she became professionally involved with Dr William Phelps, a pioneer in the treatment of spastic, or cerebral-palsied children. Though lacking medical qualifications, Eirene Collis discovered in herself a flair amounting to genius for this work. Phelps had been one of the first specialists to grasp that cerebral palsy, usually caused by damage to the brain at birth, did not necessarily involve any loss of intelligence. Children, many of whom were wrongly diagnosed as 'mentally backward' and written off by doctors, could be treated with physiotherapy and helped in several cases to lead a reasonably normal life. At that period the orthodox approach pursued by most hospital specialists was to do nothing, leaving the children to become more and more immobile and then operating when it was too late to do anything else. Thanks to the advances in anaesthetics it had become relatively easy to perform operations of this sort on spastic children. Obturator nerves were cut, adductors divided, steel appliances used to straighten out deformities. Eirene Collis deplored these developments. She advocated instead a return to the approach of William John Little who, in a memorable paper *On the Influence of Abnormal Parturition etc on the Mental and Physical Condition of the Child* (1862) first established the link between cerebral palsy and difficulties experienced by the mother in labour. Little taught that the best results were obtained not by surgery, of the type so vividly described by Flaubert, when Monsieur Bovary operates on Hippolyte Tautain's club foot by cutting his Achilles' tendon, but by a treatment 'based upon physiology and rational therapeutics' – what we would now call physiotherapy. Her methods depended on teaching children to re-use and re-educate muscles affected by deformity. This meant involving parents, and in particular the patient's mother. 'The mother,' she wrote, 'should be in the centre of the picture, fully responsible for day-to-day management of the child under guidance. The function of everybody else concerned is to advise her in humility in the job which only she and the child can carry out.' Helped only by her determination and her dynamic personality she single-handedly set to work at Queen Mary's Hospital for Children at Carshalton on 1 January 1943. To begin with she had only six children and worked in one of the hospital wards. She herself virtually lived in the ward. Meals were sent up to her from the kitchen and she ate with the children, observing them all the time. She often worked over the weekends, again, in these early days, single-handed. Gradually the number of patients increased as she won the respect of doctors who, while suspicious of her methods, could not ignore the results she achieved, often with children whom they had dismissed as helpless cases. They began to refer children to her for diagnosis. 'It was noticeable,' Collis wrote with pride,

how doctors with theory, but lacking the intuitional flair which Eirene possessed, would turn to her for a ruling. Thus if they were confronted with a child about whom they were dubious as to whether he or she was mentally deficient or a victim of cerebral palsy though perfectly intelligent, they would not be always able to decide. But Eirene could decide at a glance and give an instant ruling, greatly to the relief of everyone.

Eventually she established a special unit of her own, children being sent to her from all over the country for diagnosis and treatment. She began to lecture and travel abroad, helping to start clinics similar to her own in Dublin and Italy. Every working moment of her life was from now on devoted to her patients, some of whom she loved like a mother. Her own children and her husband took second place.

So for four years, from 1943 to 1947, the Collises lived apart as they had before the war, both pursuing their separate vocations, he as a farm labourer, she as a medical pioneer. But in 1947 their two daughters, now in their teens, returned from America, where they had been at boarding school, and Collis was faced with a dilemma. He could either stay put doing the farm work he so much enjoyed, or he could give it all up to be with his wife and children. He chose the latter course, with the result, again, that the course of his life was dramatically altered.

It may be that the recent success of *While Following the Plough* and *Down to Earth* had eased the tension between husband and wife, much of which was caused by her exasperation at his lack of success. She had always wanted him to be acclaimed. And now his two books, which she herself perhaps recognised as being on a different level from anything he had done before, had met with at least some form of recognition. Both had been excellently reviewed and had been reprinted. *Down to Earth* even won a prize, the Heinemann Foundation Award for Literature, which was presented to Collis by Lord Wavell. All this may well have persuaded Eirene that the tide had at last turned for her neglected husband and that they could try to make a fresh start.

Perhaps Collis, too, thought that things might now be different. But what had bound him to Eirene before the war – her dependence on him due to illness – was no longer a factor. She was now an independent woman who could get on quite well without him. Whatever feeling of obligation he might have had towards her in the past had gone. But his daughters were different. Collis felt guilty about the fact that they had spent their early years in poverty, years in which he had failed to provide any more than their most basic needs. In the nearest he ever came to expressing remorse about anything, he wrote:

There is no question as to the truth of this: the time to make the best of your children, and unquestionably the time when they enjoy your company best, is before the age of ten. I realise that I am stating the obvious and that I am preaching; but I have a firm grasp of the obvious when it is too late. We should always listen carefully to the man who preaches what he has not practised. HE is the man to attend to, not the good man, who so seldom feels the urge to preach. I do not say that I wholly failed in this. 'Tell us a story, Daddy,' they would plead in bed in the evening, and on the spot I would begin 'There was a hare who . . .' and would blindly carry forward – successfully enough for the insistence of another instalment next evening. But I am far from sure whether to have not entirely failed when one could have wholly succeeded does not make matters worse when the opportunity has passed and the children have ceased to care.

Like all Collis's personal passages this one is confused, and conveys the impression of a man struggling to say something that he cannot quite bring himself to say. What it amounts to is that he is trying to apologise to his daughters for neglecting them during their childhood and from it one can deduce that the main reason for his giving up his farm job and sacrificing a way of life that was ideally suited to him, was so that he could make amends, especially now that their mother was doing a full-time job and was wholly absorbed with the handicapped. Collis was a moral man, with a firm sense of right and wrong; though, like many men, he persuaded himself that morality did not enter into relationships with women. He might have left his wife at this point, on the simple grounds that she had no need of him, but he could not bring himself to abandon his daughters. So the Collis's, like many parents before and since, stayed together, 'for the sake of the children'. And staying together meant staying in Surrey, so that Eirene could be near her place of work. As is so often the case the children derived little benefit from the reunion – the atmosphere in their new home was unhappy. Their parents, who met one another only at mealtimes, were always quarrelling. As soon as they could, both girls married, and left home. The younger, Gabrielle, had never got on with Collis while Elizabeth further offended him by becoming a Jehovah's Witness and was only reunited with him shortly before his death.

Would his life have been different if he had stayed in Dorset? Having made his choice, Collis persuaded himself that it would not have altered anything. His years on the land, he said, had given him certain insights which enabled him to pursue at last his proper vocation, which was to write about natural phe-nomena. He concocted an alibi to cover a course that had been dictated by conscience: from now on his farming days were seen merely as a prelude, a starting-off point.

But regularly for the rest of his life Collis would re-visit those Dorset scenes where he had seen his Vision of Glory. He looked in at Hannan's farm, finding it all unchanged even after the death of 'E. He wandered through Collis' Piece marking the growth of the ash trees that he had planted. One evening in the summer of 1962, when he was driving up Win Green Hill near where he used to work, he stopped the car to look at the view as he always did, and saw in a nearby field a farm worker loading the harvest of wheat single-handed – driving his tractor from stook to stook, loading it, then getting back into the tractor, and so on. Acting, as always, on impulse, Collis jumped over the fence, went up to the man and offered to help him. Much to his surprise the tractor driver agreed:

By good chance I happened to have a pair of boots in the car and a mackintosh jacket. I went and put them on and joined him. I climbed onto the wagon with a prong and said I would load. The loader receives sheaves pitched up to him and arranges them on the wagon. If he doesn't do his part of the job properly and *build* his wagon-load almost as carefully as if he were building a rick, there will soon be an inextricable mess of sheaves on the wagon ready to fall off and with no room for any more. I have no natural aptitude for seizing the best way of doing a thing, but once it is pointed out to me (nearly always just commonsense), I am inclined to do it rather better than the profession-als – being more fresh and keen. I like loading a wagon and, quick with my prong in dealing with sheaves, can build a load that will not topple over as the tractor draws it along over uneven ground. In a minute or so the labourer saw that I knew my business, all was easy between us, and together we erected a high wagon-load of wheat sheaves. I overdid it though, and as we approached the rick over some bad ruts, the pile swayed and trembled but did not actually fall over. So I didn't lose face.

We now pitched up to the rick, everyone in a good mood, even the boss who appeared. He could not make me out, and no doubt wondered if he would have to pay me. It was an exceptionally lovely summer's evening; the clouds that gathered round the setting sun turned to rose, the white road grew whiter and the dark copse darker. We finished the rick before it became too dark, and shaking friendly hands all round I went away.

There is something very moving and even tragic about this incident, with Collis climbing over the fence and for an hour or two re-entering the world where he had once experienced so much happiness. With his usual reticence, he says nothing about his feelings beyond repeating what he had often said before about the pleasure of being a participator rather than a spectator of the rural scene. We can only guess at his intense emotion as in the gathering dark he said goodbye, got in his car and drove away:

> That is the land of lost content
> I see it shining plain
> The happy highways where I went
> And cannot go again.

VII

Collis had almost literally buried himself. Ewell was a backwater and there was nothing remarkable about 54 West Street, an ivy-covered suburban house dating from the 1920s with hung tiles, leaded windows and a large unkempt garden at the back. In this unpromising setting he reverted to his hermit ways. Apart from the Ewell Tennis Club, of which he became an enthusiastic member, he played little part in the social life of 'the village', as the more aspiring inhabitants like to refer to it. Occasionally he visited the local pub, the Spring Hotel, where John Osborne's mother had once worked as a barmaid. But the regulars never knew quite what to make of him. He disconcerted one drinker who told him a dirty joke by saying 'But *why* were the Englishman, the Irishman and the Jew in the restaurant? They obviously had nothing in common.' Apart from two or three disciples who knew his books and relied on him for help and encouragement, he saw hardly anyone.

As if to emphasise his isolation, Collis established his workplace in a greenhouse-cum-shed at the bottom of the garden. Here, in all but the worst of weather, he retreated from the demands of his wife and children, from the telephone, from noise and nuisances of all kinds. 'To find John on even quite bad days,' writes his Ewell friend Alan Betts, 'it was usual to squeeze past the vegetation and go round the back of the house. It was no use knocking at the front door – the bell didn't work. At the end of the garden he would emerge from the bushes like Ben Gunn, often dressed only in shorts in weather when most people were wearing sweaters.' Collis did much of his writing out of doors. Everyone who visited the Ewell house pictures him in his shed. Phoebe Merricks who, as the mother of a cerebral palsied son, knew Eirene Collis before she met John, was only just aware that she had a husband: he was somebody living a separate existence at the bottom of the garden. And if anything symbolised the change in Collis's way of life it was this garden. Was it not to be expected that a man who had written so eloquently about the potato would carry on the good work in his own back yard? He did not, and it became a wilderness in which nettles and docks thrived and straggly shrubs grew unpruned.

As his wife became more successful, Collis sank further and further into obscurity. He continued to write, but his books were largely ignored by reviewers and sold fewer and fewer copies. Eirene's success only seemed to make things worse for him. It was in a way reminiscent of his elder brother Maurice, who had taken up writing in later life and achieved immediate acclaim. Collis had marked himself down as the genius in the family, but first his brother and now his wife had achieved unexpected recognition for their work – his wife was even honoured by the Italian government.

Their roles had been reversed. Collis could no longer condescendingly address her, as he had done before the war, as if she was a poor helpless little thing incapable of survival without his support, incapable of appreciating his struggle to fulfil his destiny. Now the person who had a destiny to fulfil was Eirene. She lived for her work, and fought for the acceptance of her ideas. If anyone beat a path to the door of 54 West Street, Ewell, the chances were that they had come to see her, not him. To complete the reversal, Eirene was earning a regular wage. He had become dependent on her for what little money they had, and she rubbed it in. Even when she bought a car, she refused to let Collis use it.

The situation certainly did not inspire self-confidence. As he wrote to Martyn Skinner: 'When I was neglected from 1947 to 1970 I ceased to believe in my stuff, for one's friends begin to disbelieve in one also, and as for one's family!!! There were times when I wondered that I could even sign my name.'

During these dismal years Collis wrote seven books in all, which divide themselves into two groups – scientific and biographical. The scientific were *The Triumph of the Tree*, *The Moving Waters* and *Paths of Light*; the biographical *An Artist of Life: Havelock Ellis, Marriage and Genius, Tolstoy: A Pictorial Biography* and *The Carlyles*. The three scientific books were later abridged in a one-volume version, *The Vision of Glory*.

I do not propose in this short book to provide a detailed appreciation of Collis's scientific books. He himself, along with many of his most enthusiastic critics, regarded them as his finest work. They seek to re-interpret the findings of scientists in unscientific and occasionally poetical language. For this purpose Collis taught himself science – an extraordinary thing for a man of his age to do. He set up his one-man university and strove to master the discoveries of the physicists so that he could describe in his own words what photosynthesis meant or what happens when the atom is split. There was something heroic about this task, yet to the reader who has enjoyed Collis's farming books *The Vision of Glory* will come as a disappointment. The explanation is simple. Whereas before Collis had been writing from personal experience, now he was re-working the writing of others. He had become no more than an inspired translator, his books being – in Arthur Calder-Marshall's words – 'digests, WEA lecture pieces without any original research, but polished to the brilliance of gems'.

That is a harsh judgment but it is a just one, and it explains why, when republished, *The Vision of Glory* never achieved the success of *While Following the Plough*. All the same, there was the 'brilliance of gems' which Calder-Marshall noticed, the use of prose to transform science into poetry:

We take a piece of coal in our hands, a black stone. It is carbon, it is sunshine shaped into a solid. It is a piece of the sun itself we hold, the blazing ball itself turned into the dirty darkness of that rock. It may be very cold, freezing to the touch on a winter's day: yet still it is the ancient furnace that we finger, it is heat made cold, a frozen burning beam. We do not doubt this for a minute. We know how to change it back again. We put a piece of its own element in touch with it – its own essence, flame – and in a few minutes the box files open and the trebly millioned years imprisoned sun streams out, and the ransomed rays that fell upon the ferns fall on us today.

Collis spent many hours in his shed polishing these Ruskinian phrases and he was very proud of them – prouder, perhaps, because of the greater effort that was required than when, say, writing about backing a horse and cart through a narrow gateway. But if they shine it was not because of mere Irish rhetoric on Collis's part. He was genuinely excited by what he unearthed in his research. He told me:

I could look at phenomena and realise that if I did do so with any care, with any intensity, then I would find that natural phenomena were simply stuck through with mystery, hyperbole and paradox; that fields are simply fallen mountains, for instance, that mountains are the seas of further continents, that coal is simply squashed trees; that oil is squashed fish; that chalk is squashed skeletons of shell-fish; as for a dunghill, well that's a poem in itself. As for the atom, people talk about the atom very lightly don't they? They talk about 'splitting the atom', but no one has ever split the atom. What you do is you open the atom and you find an atom within the atom, and when you've found the atom within the atom you don't find an atom at all. You find something else. You find a *tiger* jumping out in the form of energy. So that mass, apparently, is the same as energy and energy the same as mass. You can't get more hyperbolical than that. And you're not talking rubbish, because the moment somebody says 'No, no. When you've opened your little box no tiger's going to spring out,' you can immediately take such a box and open it and destroy a city.

In his biographical books, Collis wrote almost as much about marriage as he had written about nature. The relationship between husband and wife seemed almost to obsess him. He wrote a book called *Marriage and Genius*, which was an account of the married lives of Strindberg and of Tolstoy. He returned again to the subject of Tolstoy in *Tolstoy: A Pictorial Biography* – a book which was never put on sale as the publishers, Burns and Oates, went out of business at the very time it was due to appear, another typical bit of Collis bad luck; and again, in *The Carlyles* he focussed his attention on another ill-matched pair, Thomas and Jane Welsh Carlyle. In each case he seems to have chosen his subect because he, or she, was unhappily married.

Talking on the subject, Collis loved to quote a line from *John*

Bull's Other Island, which he remembered from the first time he had ever seen a play by Bernard Shaw – 'He's come to *torment* you, and you're driven already to *torment* him.' Collis quoted this to me in a stage Shavian accent, adding with a laugh 'Ever since that day to this I've never seen men and women do anything else.' In *Marriage and Genius* he wrote: 'Husbands and wives do not love each other very much as a rule. The circumstances are against it.' In the cases of Strindberg and Tolstoy Collis couldn't help blaming the wives:

Some purely feminine ·women, sacrificing self to an extraordinary degree, are content to use themselves entirely as wives and mothers: this their complete vocation, this their art and labour of love . . . But not a great many forceful women are content with this role. They too often seek the domination which spreads terror rather than peace and joy. This tragedy queen act is a genuine secret and few men have ever known how to meet it.

With this pessimistic but not unusual view of marriage went another, rather more idiosyncratic, theory that marriage, or 'the matrimonial struggle', as he called it, is a highly secret affair between a man and a woman. 'Few of us,' he said, 'know much about the married life of even our closest friends. Nothing is guarded so secretly as this matter.' But a moment's reflection about his remark is enough to expose its falsity to experience. However much people may try, marriages cannot be conducted secretly. There are children, and in the old days there were servants. Again, a great many men and women do not want to keep their marriages private. They confide in friends, often to excess, not only about their troubles but about their pleasures. They write letters and diaries; they make telephone calls. As

Collis knew perfectly well from his study of the Tolstoys, the result is that some marriages are even better documented than many public and historical events.

The reason he wrote in this way was that he wanted his own marriage to be a secret. He cared about it so much that he persuaded himself that *all* marriages are secret, although, if that had been the case, he could never have written his biographies.

In all our conversations, Collis never mentioned his first wife. In all his correspondence with Martyn Skinner over twelve years, she is not once referred to.

Why did they marry? If we turn for enlightenment to his autobiography we find this paragraph:

I sometimes hear people say that they are bored at reading about love affairs in autobiographies. I am not bored by this myself, but I find it impossible to write about it – and that's flat. Early in my twenties I became engaged, but the girl was much too sensible to keep it up. Later I was to be married to an American girl. She had to return to America (or I let her return) and then she wrote to me in Dorset from New York to say that she did not wish to marry me. I borrowed – rather I was given by a kind friend – the passage money and took the boat to America to see if I could get her back. I was unsuccessful . . . Shortly after this I met my wife in London and got married after a week.

It really is extraordinary the way people talk about marriage etc. etc.

There then follows a short essay, in general terms, on the subject of marriage.

In all Collis's writing there is no more extraordinary passage than this one. As so often with his personal memories, it is not only evasive but inaccurate. According to Stephen Potter, in the unpublished part of his autobiography, Collis was engaged not once but twice: on the first occasion to Margaret Lindsay, the sister of Sir Kenneth Lindsay: and secondly to an unnamed 'girl in Barnet'. Perhaps the most extraordinary thing about it is the way in which, on a quick reading, its significance can easily be overlooked. I don't remember myself registering, when I first read the book, that Collis married his wife, *having known her for only a week*. None of the reviewers mentioned this unusual event. It is so casually dropped in, at the end of a paragraph in which the American girl is the main point of interest that if Collis had written 'I murdered her after a week' one wonders how many readers would have noticed.

Looking at it again, one sees that the most significant thing about that sentence is the silence at the end of it. Having told the world that he was married after a week, Collis does not go on to say, as most people do who tell you of a 'whirlwind romance', that he never regretted his decision for a minute. He says nothing at all. He proceeds to deliver a little homily, in his usual laconic vein, on the subject of marriage. As so often with Collis the effect is both comic and tragic. It is comic that a man who marries a woman he has known for a week should regard himself as a suitable expert on the subject of marriage; it is tragic that he is so proud, and so ashamed, that he cannot unburden himself of his true feelings about his wife.

As it happens, one can fill in some of the gaps with the help of the unpublished novel, *Progress of an Artist*. It is clear from comparing certain passages in this book with Collis's own memoirs that it is undisguised autobiography – a fact that makes it unacceptable as a novel. But as a means of throwing some light on Collis's early life and loves it is a valuable document. From it one can confirm the impression of his skimpy, paragraph in *Bound Upon a Course* that he not only married the wrong woman, but failed to marry the right one. His American girl he calls 'Marion' – her real name was Elizabeth – and praises 'her irreplaceable calmness and poise and warmth and loveableness and generosity of attitude'. As for himself, he writes, in the third person, very objectively about his immaturity:

He didn't know much about women. With Marion he had wonderful happiness and amity. He didn't know that no-one finds another human being with whom he experiences continual amity. Few find it once. That was the first error he made. He made another also which is common and yet unbelievable. When the love ecstasy had passed he thought it ought not to pass. He wanted the *thrill* to be kept up . . . He made a third elementary error. He was not continuously in love with Marion. He thought he ought to be. He thought that if he was in love, in kissing love, at 2 p.m., he ought to be at 4 p.m. and he felt annoyed that he wasn't always. He was the victim of a fourth error. He thought that beautiful women were continuously beautiful. He was not experienced enough to know the changes, the transcendent changes in the appearance of all women at various times of the day.

'Marion' wanted to marry Collis, but Collis shied away. This was the British Museum period of his life when he was setting out, under the influence of G. B. Edwards, to follow his destiny. 'Evidently he did not want to marry at this time,' he says of his fictional self. 'That's all it came to.' But later on he adds, 'He was against the idea of marriage. He was instinctively terrified of it. This went very deep. To keep clear of marriage at present had been a rooted motive within him ever since his engagement. He was afraid that if he married he wouldn't get his work done.'

Typically, having set his face against marriage, Collis suddenly changed his mind. He determined to marry Marion and pursued her to New York. But it was too late. She had fallen in love with another man. He pleaded with her but it was no use. There were tears on both sides and Collis quoted Othello:

> . . . of one whose hand
> Like the base Indian, threw a pearl away
> Richer than all his tribe

Then:

He went home. A wave of gloom passed into him. Neither while in America, nor when coming from America, nor immediately after getting home, did he remember Marion as clearly and as continually as he did now. Ah, if only he had sometimes fought with her and been unhappy – then he could feel well quit of the unhappy times, but they had never fought . . . If only he could forgive himself and recognise – as somewhere in his mind he did – the inevitability of what had happened. But he could not forgive himself: for though some may forgive others their trespasses unto seven times seven, no man will forgive himself for the very thing that he would do again . . .

She had given him a gramophone. Had she wished to have been avenged upon him for his neglect, nothing could have served better than that gift. Music heard at one special time and in one special place carries in its voice the memory of that time and the picture of that place. When he put on the records that they had played together, then the old days and the old scenes would mercilessly parade before his mind . . . He frequently played one record especially 'Iphigenia Auf Tauris'. But it was wearing out. The needle almost got stuck now.

This evening he put it on again, and once more the notes carried him back to the lovely days, and he remembered how he had gone down the stairs saying – These are my golden hours. It was an old disc, recording the extraordinarily beautiful voice of Ginaida Jurjevskaja. It was irreplaceable, for it would not be re-made, nor held in the equivalent of a library – but allowed to die for ever.

He put it on a table, got a penknife, and slowly composed across it these words:

> *To this Mortal Singer*
> None speak your name
> You are dead.
> Never on earth again
> Shall you be heard
> Yet divine singer
> I hear thee still!
> Though this scratched record
> Is all that remains
> Of thy voice and thy word
> I hear thee still!

He then wrapped it up and put it away in a box beside a portrait of Marion which he possessed.

I have been unable to discover how Collis met his first wife, Eirene. The impression he gives in his autobiography is that on his return from America he decided to get married almost to the first girl he met. Certainly it happened so quickly that even his best friend Stephen Potter knew nothing about it until it was a *fait accompli*. 'Who are you married to and in what sense?' he asked in pained surprise. 'Rings? Children? Church? Why not me as best man? Why no telegrams? Cake?'

Many years later, as it happened, Collis asked Potter, who was touring in America with his second wife, Heather Jenner, to pay a call on 'Marion', now married to another man and living in New York. He reported:

I took H. to 300 Central Park. I found

1. That he, the husband, was pleasant unaffected and not very outstanding in looks and personality.

2. They have an 11th floor flat looking North and East of the Park – very surely the finest setting for any park or any flat – brilliantly and expensively decorated in completely modern dress – best absolutely contemporary decor I've seen.

3. She is obviously both beautiful and charming.

4. She showed me photographs of you. One or two things she said to me alone showed me that your relationship with her had been of the utmost importance to her, unforgettable and permanent.

It was not surprising that in the circumstances Collis's marriage turned out unhappily. Eirene may have been deeply in love with Collis when they married but as the years passed and he so singularly failed to succeed exasperation set in.

She believed in his work. But it must be successful, and it must not come before her. It was not successful and yet it did come before her. With a naturalness that rose with complete spontaneity she began to hate his work, to hate the things that would not sell, though she had once loved them. She hated to see him pile his table with books the reading of which, she thought, could not lead him anywhere. And she couldn't bear the way he wanted to study by himself, to go out, to leave her, to use the Museum as his office. She didn't want him to have an office – that is, another house – the one solution that holds together hundreds and thousands of marriages. With a naturalness that rose with complete spontaneity he revolted against this. And so they clashed – again and again. They were a match for one another, neither yielding an inch, each answering jibe with jibe, scorn with scorn, epithet with epithet, taunt with taunt. Violence was not used, for she was a weak woman and he was a strong man. Nature is provident. If women were

122

physically as strong as men the world would reek with matrimonial bloodshed and injury and death.

Collis, by nature a mild and gentle person, found himself dismayed by the ferocity, the cruelty and the egotism that Eirene provoked. Yet, he insisted – at least before the war, when he wrote his novel – that in spite of all the quarrels, their love for one another remained.

She became terrified if he was ill, or when she thought he might leave her, or when he looked like falling in love with someone else. She didn't admire him, she didn't respect him, she didn't honour him, she didn't treasure him or anything of his, she wasn't proud of him – but she loved him . . . and in spite of everything he loved her. She was so beautiful in every part of her person every hour of the day, so attractive, so dear: and when not weighed down by anything, when the sky was unclouded and she was enjoying herself, how alive, how spontaneous, how unsophisticated her expressions of pleasure – then they were *at one* and saw things with the same eye and the same understanding. Though he was never to find her calm, never indeed to walk a hundred yards with her and find her composed, he often did feel at one with her and that they alone belonged together.

Over the years, as Eirene Collis pursued her own career with more and more success, her attitude to her husband changed. She came to regard him as a total failure, speaking of him to others with complete contempt. Yet until the end he never wholly lost a spark of devotion – as is clear from what little he writes about her in *Bound Upon a Course*. I quote here the passage in which he describes his wife's last years because it illustrates so clearly his infuriating *evasiveness* when writing about personal matters and also the difficulty that confronts his biographer trying to get at the truth:

In the Fifties my wife was suddenly struck down by a cerebral thrombosis which caused her to become completely paralysed on her left side – a brain damage not dissimilar from the palsy she had for so long striven to alleviate in others ... She never recovered. No movement ever returned to her left leg or her left arm. At first it was possible for her to sit in a wheelchair, but it was terribly difficult to dress and undress her. I looked after her for six years, day and night, though I never really mastered the art of lifting her without strain. Her ordeal lasted for twelve years, the last six in a Nursing Home where I could visit her with regularity. She died while I was writing this book.

Here I must say frankly that had she died a few years previously, and had I been able to get everything into perspective I would have tried to write more fully; but as it is I find it too difficult.

She had been dying slowly before my eyes for years, yet her death came suddenly. One day she had another stroke. When I reached her she was unconscious and though it seemed that she recognised me and our daughters, I am not certain. In the evening the doctor said that until the morning it would be impossible to know what the effects of the second thrombosis would be and I was advised to go home. But instead of my telephoning early next morning, the matron rang to say that she had died in the night. I went to the nursing home, as I had gone for so many years to see the living person. I can never take reality for *less* than it is: and I have often wished that at funerals, not a closed coffin but an open one were brought into the church, the dead face visible to all. That would make people sit up and wake from the dream! At the nursing home the night before there had been the living, warm, breathing creature, and here she was now, a horizontal statue, severe, alien, unseeing and unbreathing, as cold as marble, and totally unin- terested in communicating a single word. Anything – anything but

124

this! I felt. I do not know if time will soften this harsh scene for me, but I doubt it. Of course it was a release for her, and I had been horrified by the thought that she might still have to suffer more and worse hardship. My friends thought that it would be a release for me as well as for her. But the heart of man is not only desperately wicked but desperately complicated. I *had* thought it would be a release for me. I had thought that it would be a relief not to have to walk through the dreary corridor to her room week after week, that I would be glad to be free. I never told her that I would miss her and choke with tears every time I *should* have been getting ready to go to her and bring her things. And she did not know this. She always managed to get me wrong, and I made no effort for her to get me right, for I did not know my own heart, I did not know that when the time came I would not be able to bear her *non-existence*. She read a lot of paperbacks. I decided to sort them out and put aside a number for the nursing home library. Shortly after the funeral I brought them in. This was a mistake. Going in and giving the books to a sister, I found a terrible strain. As swiftly as could be I unpacked the books, unable to speak a word, and *fled* from the place with clenched fists. And it is because of this, and because of the words unspoken and the sorrow unknown that time may not soften or heal the harshness of that final scene.

What is all that supposed to be about, the reader may find himself asking. There is no questioning the feeling, the passion almost, of the writer; but what is he trying to tell us with his 'words unspoken and sorrow unknown', not to mention the 'desperately wicked heart of man'? Some things are clear enough, but otherwise it gives a powerful sense of an enormous well of emotion stoppered up by that short central paragraph: 'Here I must say frankly that had she died a few years previously, and had I been able to get everything into perspective

I would have tried to write more fully: but as it is I find it too difficult.'

Collis is using the fact of his wife's recent death as an excuse not to tell the true story. A mixture of grief, remorse and pride – the dominant emotion – prevents him from being open about himself. Yet even when he is concerned with mere facts, as in the description of his wife's death, he is dishonest – as the letter quoted below confirms.

The truth of the matter, as far as I can glean it, is this: the relationship between John and Eirene Collis had deteriorated to such an extent that by 1957 they had finally decided to separate. Their children had grown up and left home. Eirene had a lover, a young doctor colleague at her hospital, and Collis took this very badly. Although he had many casual affairs with women, he insisted, like a lot of men, on thinking that a wife's infidelity was on a different level of seriousness to a husband's. Yet it was precisely at this moment when they had finally come to their decision to separate that Eirene had her stroke. Collis could not now abandon her. He could have forced her into a nursing home, but he did not. Instead, for the next twelve years, he stayed at her side, looking after her as best he could and impressing on all who witnessed it the gentleness with which he nursed her. Throughout her long years of illness, frustrated by the inactivity, she remained implacably hostile towards him and he would often return shaking from his hospital visits because she had been so unpleasant. One can find a veiled reference to this in remarks Collis made in a *Spectator* review about Katherine Mansfield:

When a document or a coin is invalid we declare it unsound and lay it aside. When a person is invalid through faulty physiology, we take a more lenient view, calling him or her an 'invaleed', to be treated with respect, while the person in question often tends to use that very invalidity as a licence by means of which others may be oppressed or destroyed.

If only Collis could have told this tragic story, how much more moving and effective it would have been, compared to his evasive and incomplete account. And how much more moving, in the true version, would have been his sincere expression of grief. But he could not bring himself to tell us the truth – not from grief, nor from respect for the dead, but from pride and that unnatural reticence that went back to his childhood. Only when the gaps are filled in, when we know that the man who for twelve years looked after his wife did so to the accompaniment of constant abuse and vilification; when we realise that he did so knowing at the same time that she was in love with another man; only then can we appreciate his heroism and glimpse his true stature.

VIII

His situation now, in 1970, was very desperate. He was seventy years old, his wife was dead, his two daughters estranged from him, there was no sign that his work would gain any recognition. He was, as always, short of money, reduced to working in the Post Office at Christmas to supplement his earnings from lecturing. And yet such was the extraordinary nature of his life, that only four years later Collis's circumstances were utterly transformed. He was married again, to a woman who was devoted to him, he was materially well off, his books had been acclaimed and were about to be republished, and for the rest of his life he was to enjoy success and happiness. His prophetic wish, expressed so many years before, to be a 'vigorous old man', freed from all worries, was at last fulfilled.

In a letter to Phoebe Marricks, written shortly after his marriage in September 1974 at the age of seventy, Collis – for once writing from the heart – poured out his feelings:

I have received very pleasant letters from friends after my marriage. But your letter was so dear, so sweet, that I could not read it without tears. It has all been somewhat of a fairy story, utterly unexpected, unhoped. In all she is, and does, and says, she is in my eyes perfect.

I call her Marina. But that is not her name. It is Irene! So I have elected to call her by another name – especially as she is the opposite to Eirene in every particular, without a singular exception.

I had to try and find among my papers Eirene's death-certificate at

West Street the other day – for I was required to produce it for official purposes. And I could not find it. It was April 6th 1970. But I had purposely not remembered the day because on that day I was enjoying April sunshine in the far end of the garden, and *did not hear the telephone* ringing and ringing from the Virginia Water Nursing Home to tell me that she was dying . . . I could not now find that certificate for I had not wished to remember that date. Looking for it the other day, tears streamed down my face and I could not assuage them. How strange is life, how strange are we! – for she had not been loving and kind to me at any time ever, she had been very, very unkind.

And now, suddenly, all is changed, and all the tears of my life are wiped away.

Collis's second wife, Irene – he soon dropped the 'Marina' – was the widow of Sir Edward Beddington Behrens, a financier and art collector who had built himself a secluded home at Abinger Common complete with tennis court and swimming pool, looking out onto paddocks and pine trees. Irene, or Renee as he called her, was Sir Edward's first cousin. They had wanted to marry when they were young but both their families were opposed and so they parted, each subsequently marrying other partners and each subsequently getting divorced. They met again by chance when Beddington Behrens was in his sixties and were married for ten years before his death in 1968. Irene, a highly intelligent and cultured woman, had studied singing and piano at the Royal College of Music and also translated the early novels of Françoise Sagan when they were first published in England. She met Collis when he drove over to Abinger one day for tea with a mutual friend. He stayed to swim in the pool. Later he returned to swim and also to read poetry to her. It became a habit and after a few months they decided to marry. Looking back, he told Skinner: 'She was far from being a lonely widow looking for a husband: nor was I looking for a wife but it has turned out that way . . . a marvellous person.'

For the first time in his life Collis now experienced domestic peace, and also comfort. Since his first wife died he had been living in one room of the Ewell house 'like a mouse'. Irene was dismayed to find that, as far as clothes were concerned, he owned only one suit, two shirts and an Old Rugbeian tie. She persuaded him to have a new suit and an overcoat made at Burton's. He was also able finally to dispense with his old Morris, which was literally falling to pieces, and buy a second-hand Renault. Though he had never set any store by physical comforts there is no doubt that in his old age he was greatly appreciative of the improvement in his living conditions. As for his wife, he had once written in *Down to Earth*: 'The great thing is to find a human being: that is, a person capable of friendship and affection and not submerged beneath class consciousness, or envy, or disappointment, or frustration, or general grudginess – and possessing life and inner warmth. We are never markedly successful in our search in any quarter.' After his experiences with his mother, his first wife and his daughters it was not surprising that he took this despairing view of human nature. What was altogether delightful and, in such a case, rare, was that during the last ten years of his life he was to know, at last, the warmth and companionship of a loving woman.

His gratitude towards her took many forms, one of which was an exaggerated courtesy, as Andrew Wilson remembers:

131

The most touching manifestation of it was that, though addicted to tobacco, he would not smoke in her company; and asked Clare Asquith and me when we went to lunch to have our cigarettes in the car and in a pub *before* we met Irene. So anxious was he to spare her the cigarette smoke that he *insisted* we smoke before we got there. And of course you can't smoke without a drink in your hand. So . . . we went to a pub. And in the pub, he got carried away, talking: first about the iniquity of the design of chairs, then about Carlyle, or how the capacity for awe is not given to children. You point up to the stars. And the child thinks 'Oh, yes those are the stars', taking them completely for granted, whereas a man is awestruck. Anyway, after all the smoking, we arrived home hours late for lunch, and Irene was obviously a bit cross, but chiefly worried.

Collis's fortunes as a writer were changed by the publication in 1971 of his autobiography *Bound Upon a Course*. Encouraged by Stephen Potter, he had started it in November 1969, five months before the death of his wife, and finished it very quickly as if his new situation had somehow released a hidden source of energy. Perhaps the writing was therapeutic, or perhaps, more mundanely, he simply needed the money. 'I only wrote my autobiography as an act of desperation,' he told Martyn Skinner, 'and there is not much of me in it, for I'm not very forthcoming re. Self when it comes to the point.' It was perfectly true. Ever since his traumatic childhood, Collis had been buttoned up, not wanting to reveal to anyone his inner feelings. But in his autobiography he did, to some extent, unburden himself; so that although the book is more of a series of reflections and views than an account of his life, there are flashes of the real Collis in the account of his relationship with his mother and even his first wife, when his feelings come tumbling out to an almost embarrassing extent. But it is, all the same, very revealing that, for example, in the account of his wife's death, described in his poignant letter to Phoebe Merricks, he concealed the truth and concocted a story of how the hospital matron had rung to tell him that his wife had died in the night. Collis was so complicated and so proud that he did not want the world to know that he was sitting in the sun at the bottom of his garden when his wife was dying.

The book is quite shapeless. It darts about from topic to topic, with Collis pausing from time to time to deliver a little lecture on a subject that has just come to mind – nudism, the monarchy, the permissive society – with passages of autobiography breaking in as though he feels duty-bound to say something about himself if only to maintain the purpose of the book as a memoir. The most unusual thing to emerge was the way in which he had stuck to his calling: 'Ever since I grew up,' he said, by way of explaining the title of his book, 'I have always felt myself bound upon a course determined less by outer circumstances than by inner impulse which I have blindly followed.' If he had shaped his book more skilfully, if he had opened up just a little further, the reader would have seen how remarkable was the way in which he had persevered at what he was doing at any stage in his life, convinced that it was fulfilling a purpose; convinced too that, at some time, his hour would come. Long ago he had been struck by a sentence in Wasserman's life of Columbus:

It is extraordinarily striking to observe how a great man's star draws him, as though by never-failing magnetic force, to his appointed end:

and whatever he does or whatever he fails to do, every error, every neglect, every apparent defeat does actually and inevitably bring him nearer to the hour of fulfilment.

It was a sign of how little in the way of recognition Collis had achieved in a lifetime of writing that his autobiography was rejected by twelve publishers before being at last accepted by Sidgwick and Jackson, thanks to the persistence of Michael Holroyd who acted as unpaid agent for the book. It was published in May 1971 and very extensively and favourably reviewed. 'He is essentially a lone original,' John Raymond wrote in the *Sunday Times*, 'an "old soul" in the Blakean sense, a seeker – and finder – of a most unusual kind. His autobiography – passionate, poetic, question-begging, strangely practical in its assumptions about life, sharp in divination, is an altogether extraordinary performance.' Arthur Calder-Marshall in the *Evening Standard* called Collis 'the most neglected master of English prose living today' and his book 'a fascinating auto-biography'. 'Why is it,' Michael Holroyd asked in *The Times*, 'that Mr Collis is not required reading?' Holroyd later named *Bound Upon a Course* as his 'Book of the Year' in *The Times*.

Holroyd, who became a close friend, was one of a small circle of admiring critics that Collis had acquired over the years and whose encouragement – in the absence of large sales – was the only proof that his opinion of himself was shared by others. ('I am John Stewart Collis,' he announced to his Ewell neighbour Alan Betts at their first meeting. 'I have been called the greatest prose writer since Ruskin.' Betts was so startled by this unusual introduction from a man he met in his local that he never forgot it.) His friend Stephen Potter, who was responsible for the comparison, was also a pillar of the Collis fan club, once nominating him as a leading member of 'a Shadow Cabinet of writers waiting to step forward when taste has changed or when judgment has become more settled'. Bernard Levin, Philip Toynbee and Dervla Murphy were among those who regularly reviewed his books with enthusiasm. His most discerning admirer and supporter was Arthur Calder-Marshall. They first met in 1958 when both were working on books to celebrate the centenary of Havelock Ellis. Collis became a family friend, finding in the Calder-Marshall household the love and affection that he had craved for and missed in his own. 'My two daughters,' Calder-Marshall writes, 'provided him with an opportunity to show the love for children he couldn't feel for his own; and my wife was the sort of mother he would have liked to have had.'

Collis spent a great deal of time cultivating this small and select band of admirers. When other people did so little to promote him, he did his best to promote himself. He sent out inscribed copies of his books. He wrote to everyone he could think of to alert them to any radio or television appearance. He didn't want anyone to miss anything he did. The lengths to which he was prepared to go in order to get noticed by the right kind of people were revealed in one of his letters to Martyn Skinner:

The thing is that there are two fellows Grigson and Rayner Heppenstall who make it a point of honour to denigrate any rival of their sort of approach – wrong word, perhaps 'age group'. They both write prose and poetry, and it is a job to determine whether their prose is worse than their poetry or their poetry worse than their prose – (and I say this seriously). Anyway when I wrote *Bound Upon a Course* I wondered how I could protect myself from them. I looked up their works to find something to quote appreciatively. I found one in a book by Heppenstall. Difficult to find any real book at all from Grigson. But I did find something about William Morris in the *Listener* and quoted it. Result: Grigson did review the book and did not slate it. It was in the *T.L.S.* unsigned. But unmistakable Grigson on account of its prose clumsiness *and* because he said: 'But Mr Collis is not always reliable on facts.' Now in my book I had told how, when lost somewhere in Dorset, unable to find my way, as a cold April day closed down, I knocked at a solitary house, to ask the way. A woman came to the door and said *'Himmler is dead.'* In my book I said I had often thought of how Wordsworth had once as he walked on the public way in Westmorland, seen a man from afar off, who as he advanced, cried out 'Robespierre is dead!' And I said to myself as I left that house in the cold sharp evening air of April, after hearing that woman say 'Himmler is dead' – 'This is good enough.'

Grigson spent a paragraph of a very short review pointing out that this Wordsworth incident happened not in Westmorland but in the lowlands of Scotland at low tide (not high tide).

PS I meant to add what my reply is to those who ask why I should seek to placate a couple of fellows of that kind. Well, I always say I do it in the spirit of a man who while climbing a tree throws a sugar plum or a nut to a monkey who seems about to bite his leg.

The favourable reception of *Bound Upon a Course* had one very beneficial consequence. The publisher Charles Knight, again encouraged by Michael Holroyd, decided to reissue some of Collis's earlier works. *A Vision of Glory*, a compilation of his three 'scientific' books, was published in 1972, and was chosen by four critics – Calder-Marshall, Holroyd, Levin and Maurice Wiggin as their 'Book of the Year'. It was followed in 1973 by

The Worm Forgives the Plough, consisting of his two farming books in one volume. Nothing gave Collis greater satisfaction than this. For it was one thing to gather 'golden opinions' over the years from a select band of critics, but if his best work was unavailable they did little to instil self-confidence. 'A great work is always re-discovered,' Collis had once written; and now, as if to prove his own greatness, here was *While Following the Plough* finding its way into print again after twenty-seven years. Nor was this the end of the story. In 1975 Penguin Books published both *The Vision of Glory* and *The Worm Forgives the Plough*, the latter remaining in print until Collis's death nine years later, having sold nearly 40,000 copies. (In addition, he was delighted to be asked, on two occasions, to appear on television, being interviewed by Bernard Levin and Joan Bakewell.)

No doubt the growth of interest in 'ecology' during the Seventies had something to do with the re-discovery of Collis, not to mention the vogue for the countryside and self-sufficiency. But although he shared many of the concerns of the ecologists, with pollution, for example, he was never in the least bit nostalgic about the countryside. He recognised that the kind of farm he had described in *While Following the Plough* had gone for good. 'Some of the labourers, are exchanged for metal,' he had written, 'while those who are not exchanged continue to work for exactly the same hours as before. I do not complain of this – I make no tirade against it. It is so much in the nature of things.' Collis looked at these issues from the personal, not the political point of view. Similarly with that other great public preoccupation of his last ten years, unemployment. In itself, he maintained, it was not necessarily a bad thing. It meant more leisure for everyone. If there was a problem about unemployment it was simply that men were quite unfitted to make use of this greater amount of leisure. He would have agreed with Orwell when he asked 'If a man cannot enjoy the return of spring, why should he be happy in a labour-saving Utopia?' Similarly with old people, a favourite hobby horse, on which he sounded a ruthless Shavian note:

Nowadays we are always being told about the miseries of 'old people', how lonely they are, how bored, how they have nothing to do, and so on – there is no end to the silly useless lamentation on their behalf. The truth is invariably evaded. It is *their own fault*. An educated person is never lonely; he is never bored; he never seeks a pastime; he can never live long enough to study all the books he has not had time for in his life. If at the age of sixteen, seventeen or eighteen a person elects to be a boor and a bore, then at the age of sixty, seventy, or eighty he will be far worse off than an old horse or an old goat or an old pig and they are never to be observed wallowing in self-pity.

Another thing he disliked about some old people was their habit of 'mellowing'. He was once talking to Andrew Wilson about Alexandra, the youngest of Tolstoy's daughters, who, after a lifetime of taking her father's side in the matrimonial war, came in old age to sympathise with her mother. Convinced that she should have gone to her grave in a fury of hatred for her mother Collis said 'in the end she *mellowed*, which was a bad thing to do. You'll never *mellow*. I'll never *mellow*.' (Collis put this down to his not being English, insisting, against the evidence, that Wilson, his fellow non-mellower, could not be English either.)

IX

In writing about old age Collis again had himself very much in mind. The thought that many old people might be frail and sick through no fault of their own did not seem to cross his mind. Just as he judged all marriages to be unhappy because his own was, so he wrote about old people as if he was a typical representative of the species rather than an extraordinary exception. It was one of the few sore points I encountered when writing about him. Usually these were very trivial things, attributable to his vanity and his desire to present a dignified front. Thus when I once described how he had read to me from his book sitting at his desk 'in stockinged feet resting on a cushion on the floor', he asked for it to be excised. He likewise took exception to my revealing that he had once made a telephone call to the *Spectator* to ask them to remove a comma from one of his book reviews.

References to his age were more upsetting. It was something I was made aware of at an early stage in our friendship. I had referred jokingly in my *Spectator* review of one of his television programmes to 'old man Collis' and he never forgot it. 'Very trying the old man Collis business,' he wrote to Martyn Skinner. 'Still I suppose I must swallow it.' He hated to be reminded of his age. When Michael Holroyd wrote in the course of his *Times* review of *Bound Upon a Course* 'He is now in his seventies and still green,' Collis minded so much that he crossed the sentence out in thick black ink. There was an occasion when another admirer, P. J. Kavanagh, met him at a *Spectator* party. Andrew Wilson had told Kavanagh that he would easily recognise Collis because 'he's very brown and looks as if he's been in an open boat for ninety years.' Kavanagh repeated this (very accurate) description to Collis and immediately regretted it because he was so obviously upset.

In an unpublished essay written shortly before his death, he said:

If anyone at any age, after twenty anyway, could be told the exact date of his death he would feel from that moment *under sentence of death* as dreadful as if pronounced by a Judge in a Court of Law: and as time went on, it would become a nightmare. And the paradox is that though we are all subject to that sentence we hardly feel it at all, simply because we don't know the date. You'd think that an old man would feel the approach of death more keenly than the younger man. But he doesn't. On the whole he continues to think that death is a long way off and carries on just as if he were at least in middle age.

One cannot be quite consistent on a subject like this. I *could* say that hardly a day passes that I don't think, one way or another, of death hovering near. But it doesn't take extreme or morbid forms. It is more of a sudden shuddering fear that I may never do this again or *see* this again. I used to think – it's all right. I've got tons of time, I'll read Gibbon's *Decline and Fall of the Roman Empire* later on in my old age, there's heaps of time. But now the dread thought occurs to me – You may have left it too late, you may never, after all, read the *Decline and Fall* (a thought I can't bear, for the style is marvellous beyond words).

And there's another thing. Now when I see young people together, I don't just see them. I have a clear vision of what they will look like and how they will behave towards each other, in twenty years' time . . .

H. G. Wells said that the tragedy of old age is not that you feel old, but that you don't. I do not accept this. I feel no tragedy in it, but an unexpected bonus. The only snag is that you don't *look* what you *feel*. Photographs are the very devil. And you are not exempt from those who refer to you as old. One of my most perspicacious critics (or flattering – the terms are synonymous for a writer) keeps referring to me as 'old man Collis'. It gives me quite a turn each time he does it. But poor chap, he's got it coming to him!

But there is one thing worse than being called an old man and that is being called 'a wonderful old man'. That hasn't happened to me yet. Perhaps I may escape it. If asked if I can account for my reasonably good health and stamina, I think I must reply – *bad teeth*. I think most modern dentists realise that teeth should be *pruned* in early days like veg. and roses. Thus there is room for them to grow and flourish with enough space. But in my youth dentists only *filled* one's close-locked teeth, using a drill slightly more alarming than the road-drills we see in the streets today. The result was that as a young man I had old or at least bad teeth that tended to poison the blood. In 1944 a dentist at Blandford, Dorset, relieved me of all my remaining teeth. One of the happiest moments of my life. From that hour I have never had a toothache nor poisoned blood therewith – nor did my dentures cause me the slightest difficulty or embarrassment for thirty years when at last they were worn down. So for good health I prescribe well-kept healthy teeth, and failing such, get rid of them.

Collis's refusal to acknowledge his age meant that he refused to talk about the things that old men are expected to talk about. To what extent he thought about them, over and above the purely dental aspect, I find it hard to say. During our taping sessions I tried to draw him out on his religion and his concept, if any, of the after-life, but he would not be drawn. As far as the after-life was concerned he would say only that 'at death we may get the surprise of our lives'. Religion to him meant living in this

141

world – not worrying about another one – and realising what an extraordinary place it is.

'If we allow our sense of beauty to grow,' he once wrote in a passage that goes far to explain his own serenity, 'we may come to find that the peculiar assurance that accompanies it is so great as to *obliterate* all other considerations.'

Collis had been brought up a Protestant in Ireland. He wrote of himself in his one published novel, *The Sounding Cataract* (1936):

He was not a Catholic. He drank the scarcely inebriating cup of Protestanism . . . He realised what a wonderful thing the Church of Rome was in Ireland, how it preserved the mystery of living and the mystery of dying, how it laid the mantle of holy words upon the daily life of the people, how it gathered them together as human beings sharing in the disaster that falls, and partaking of the glory that shines on every mortal soul.

Apart from the language of the Bible, Collis found little such nourishment in the Protestant tradition. At Rugby he responded only to certain preachers in the school chapel, especially the famous R. Studdert Kennedy: 'When I knew he was coming to preach on a given Sunday I looked forward to it with intense excitement, and when the day arrived I took my seat in Chapel with an eagerness of anticipation such as I have never experienced later in life.' These preachers were the first men to make him aware of the power of words and led him, on leaving Oxford, to think of entering the Church and becoming ordained. It was another of those episodes in his life about which he was reticent, and it is difficult to know precisely what his feelings were. His attitude to life was religious in a general sense but, remembering those sermons in Rugby chapel, what he really hankered after was preaching. In *Progress of an Artist* he described a visit to the village of Cerne Abbas before the war:

He got up and walked back through the churchyard and round to the church. He entered and closed the door behind him. He sat down in a pew enjoying the new silence and the further peace and the emptiness and the isolation. It was a dark church as all churches should be, and the windows were coloured fables adding another quiet and a still deeper calm to the motionless air.

He rose and walked up and down the aisle, then, on an impulse, mounted the pulpit steps and stood in it. He looked down at the rows of empty pews below. He placed his hands firmly on the sides of the pulpit and thought – what a marvellous place to speak from. What an opportunity for the clergyman who gets up here! If a man had anything to say, could any place on earth be so inspiring as a church pulpit? Everything was made for the orator, for the preacher, the dim light, the gentle pictures, the music, the prayer, and this firm wooden pulpit from which to speak. And then he thought of the men who now climb into these wonderful places and utter – what do they utter? He remembéred the clergyman he had last met who had been so pleased with himself for having arranged whist drives amongst his parishioners. It made life here social, he had said, it brought people together . . . These rectors had really and truly no idea that Religion might once have brought men together – as much as whist.

He stood there silent in the silence. Then – and years later he was to remember this with surprise, a sentence came to him, and he spoke out loud clearly in the empty church – *The axe must be laid to the root of the tree.*

Presumably what Collis meant by this strange text, delivered to a non-existent congregation, was that the Church in its present state would have to be cut down – though it is possible that he was also prophetically looking forward to his work as a forester in a wood not so very far from the church in which he was standing.

Collis left theological college after only a term and from then on rejected any form of Christianity. Theology became for him a dirty word, the enemy of what he considered true religion. Under the influence of Fraser's *Golden Bough*, which he had read in the British Museum, he discarded the faith he had been brought up in. But, like many who abandon Christianity, he found nothing half as good to put in its place. Encouraged by G. B. Edwards, he resorted to the pseudo-religious writings of D. H. Lawrence, Edward Carpenter – another lapsed clergyman – Count Keyserling, Walt Whitman and Havelock Ellis (about whom he wrote an unreadable book). These men preached salvation through the mystical vision, the feeling of oneness with nature. But religion cannot be understood solely in terms of nature worship, which is only a starting point. 'The beginning of truth,' said St Clement of Alexandria in the second century AD, 'is to wonder at things.' The key word is 'beginning', because wondering at things in itself can produce no ultimate revelation. Collis however persuaded himself that it could, and that the promptings of nature were all that was needed in the way of religion. He especially relied on the 'mystic experience' which a few people, not necessarily religious, are granted once, or sometimes more often, during their lives.

The mystic experience. This is surely the only ultimate. A mystic, however much and however often the word may be abused, should be

144

defined as the man who is no longer mystified – by religions, by theologies, by doctrines, by formulations. He is at ease with religions having attained Religion; he is no longer diseased by overdoses of doctrine. He occupies this favourable position by virtue of his experience which brings with it such joy and such certainty that he no longer needs dogmas about salvation: this experience to him is salvation. He no longer needs to solve the lesser problems: they have been dissolved. It may not last for more than a few minutes but it changes the man's outlook for ever – *he has seen the light*. These men are our true leaders: their goal of higher consciousness our chief hope. Their message comes down the years always with the same power to convince, always undated and undating. Their words bring continual support to the whole and the happy, and they bring hope and healing to the unhappy, to the broken in heart and even in purse, to the doubtful and the dying.

Fine words and fine phrases. Yet the game is given away when Collis goes on to instance some men who have had this mystical experience – Walt Whitman, Wordsworth, Havelock Ellis, A. J. Symonds etc. For what had they made of their mystical experience? What good had it done for Havelock Ellis, venerated by Collis as a sage and a seer? He had devoted the great part of his life to a scholarly study of sex. How could the words of such a man, however sincere, bring comfort to a dying man? The idea is absurd. Yet men other than those named by Collis have certainly brought such comfort; for example, St Paul, the writing of whose life he had turned his back on so many years before. The difference was that the seeing of the light was for him only a beginning, and not an end in itself.

The obstacle to religious faith is the ego. Men who create their own private religions, as Collis's heroes did, do so because they cannot humble themselves before God. The ego gets in the way. God is replaced by an 'inner voice' which is another word for self. What such people are looking for is a religion without tears, a religion which sweeps under the carpet such concepts as sin, prayer, forgiveness, humility and obligation, or dismisses them in a Collisian way as the preoccupations of dry-as-dust theologians.

This is not as irrevelant to Collis's career as it may seem. For a writer can only succeed if he is prepared to pursue the truth about himself, about the world and about God. To the extent that Collis deliberately closed his eyes to certain vital questions he became uninteresting and at times, as in his book on Havelock Ellis, a thundering bore. He could not progress, he could not grow wiser. 'Life, to be worthy of a rational being,' Dr Johnson wrote, 'must be always in progression: we must always purpose to do more or better than in time past.' But Collis, who had in his wartime experience been offered what he called his vision of glory, never followed the road that it opened up. Instead he convinced himself that his special calling was to write prose poetry about scientific phenomena and took himself back to what he had been doing before – library work, regurgitating the findings of others, albeit in a brilliant and memorable way.

This change of course was in part dictated by his commendable urge to rejoin his family. But it was also linked with his desire to present a front to the world and not to bare his soul. He had once written scornfully of his friend Middleton Murry, 'It is foolish to take anyone into your confidence and madness to take the public into it; but Murry did so, exposing himself all the time and frustrating the power that comes from mystery.' He could not see that he himself succeeded only when he lowered his mask; first in his wartime books, when he wrote about himself as a clumsy labourer trying to master the mechanics or as a novice uncovering the mysteries of nature; secondly in his memoirs, where in isolated passages of great power he struggled to express his real feelings about his mother and his wife. He *did* succeed, his day *did* finally come, but not in the way that he hoped. He wanted to be recognised for what he had written about the atom and about the snowflake. But people were more interested in Collis and preferred to read about his farming days. He himself could never quite accept that this was his best writing, because it meant admitting that everything he had done since marked a falling-off. He overlooked the truth of something he had written many years before: 'Men do not find that for which they search nor accomplish that which they set out to do. Search and ye shall find, Jesus said. He did not say that you would find that for which you sought. You find something else. That is the paradox of adventure.'

X

In the course of writing my profile of Collis for *People* I visited him again at Abinger Common in November 1982. I don't remember particularly what was discussed; but after lunch we both went into his study and it was there that he removed his shoes, put his feet on a cushion under the desk and read me in his soft Irish voice a passage from *While Following the Plough*:

We were now on a field beside that piece of kale I had first hoed, those plants that had seemed so poor in promise. The miserable stalks that I remembered were now as thick as a man's leg and as high as the waist or shoulders – and again I marvelled at the march. We worked very late that evening, and it was an especially lovely one. The wind had gone down completely and all the shapes of earth captured in the yellow rays were sculptured by their shades. The sun set and the dusk gathered, and with it came a deeper silence, as when a clock stops ticking in a darkened room: the clouds had got stuck and would never move again; the new moon stooped down so low above a tree that I could have hung my hat upon its horn. The final tricky part of the rick-making began when, the platform growing very narrow, I had to handle the sheaves with much circumspection. Down below I could see the roads becoming whiter and the fields darker and the woods more sombre, and as I glanced at them it occurred to me that perhaps after all this is how I would prefer to catch sight of beauty – through the corner of my eye, while immersed in something else, while not seeking it at all.

As I had been when listening to *A Book at Bedtime*, I was again struck by the power and the inspiration of his wartime writing and felt fortunate to be there listening. Later, driving home, I thought how good it would be if, before he died, Collis could be persuaded to record readings from his own work. I wrote to the BBC Radio Producer Martin Jenkins and after a lunch with his superior Piers Plowright, who knew Collis's work, he commissioned for the BBC a forty-five-minute programme to include readings and an interview in which Collis would be encouraged to talk about his life. During the summer of 1983 we had three sessions of taping. But, as so often happens with broadcasting, things did not go according to plan. Collis, who had read so well when I alone was his audience, became untypically nervous when asked to read into a tape-recorder, so the programme developed into more of a conventional interview. There was nothing wrong with that and he spoke very eloquently about his childhood, his mother, Bernard Shaw etc. All the same I realised then, I think for the first time, just how cagey he was about himself. He always disliked speaking impromptu. (Once, after he had read an address to a literary society in Rye, the Chairman of the meeting said he was sure that Mr Collis would be delighted to answer questions. But to the dismay of all he said No, he didn't want to.) For my interview, he asked me to write down all my questions in advance so that he would have time to think about his answers. This made him more fluent, but it also meant that there was very little spontaneity in the interview, and in the event he said hardly anything that he had not already written down in one or other of his books.

His desire to be word-perfect was obsessive. Right up till his death he was continuously thinking of additions and embellishments to make. He would ring up and ask if he could re-record an answer to one of my questions, as he had just thought of something new that he would like to bring in.

In October that year he drove to Lincolnshire to see his daughter Elizabeth whom he had not spoken to for ten years. It was an unusual thing to do and suggests that he may have suspected that he did not have long to live. Then on 15 December 1983 I received the following letter:

My dear Richard,
When I wrote last a propos of the radio programme, I did not mention something else. But it would be absurd for me not to mention it. Put my lack of doing so down to swiftness of events.

The fact is there was a knock on my door.

And of course the Unexpected Visitor.

My digestion has never been my strong point. But (what is now 3 weeks ago) I felt real trouble in the regions of the bowel.

So to the doctor.

'You have got jaundice. You must see a specialist at once.'

Next day I saw the specialist – a surgeon.

'You have an obstruction. Can you come into hospital tomorrow?'

'Yes.'

'We will examine you, and if desirable, *operate* on Monday.'

'Have I got gallstones – '

'No, it is more likely to be a tumour.'

'A tumour can be benign or malign, I understand.'

'Yes.'

'And a malign tumour is a polite word for cancer.'

'Yes.'

This was a very unboring dialogue, and new for me. Not my scene really. Yet bracing in a way.

Then into hospital. Questions galore and tests. Whisked about in a wheel chair through endless corridors – of powerlessness as far as I was concerned. To X Ray and Ultra Sound.

By the Friday the diagnosis. The moment of truth.

'You have a tumour. It is *malign*. It is too large to operate on and remove. But we can cure the jaundice by inserting a tube that will bypass the tumour.'

Thus my next step was an operation performed under local anaesthetic. It *failed*. So a second one, under general anaesthetic – which *succeeded*.

And now I am home again, recovering as best I can and will write again anon.

I am extremely anxious that you should take this in confidence and on no account let anyone at the BBC know. You never know, they might possibly even abandon the programme.

As far as expectation of life is concerned, I am told that at my age the growth of a tumour is *so slow* that I may well die of something else before it is ready to finish me off. This is not wishful thinking, for so many people have told me that and given me instances.

But one never knows.

Anyway, I am anxious that I am given the opportunity of *tidying up* our programme. Of saying just a sentence or so which I left out re religion, for instance. Also re prose-poetry. After all, the programme will be part of my literary remains, either in the BBC archives, or in my own taped archives, accessible whenever anyone wants to do a programme on me at any time. So please help me to satisfy myself. You have done so much already, please do this also.

It was quite difficult, even for me, to discover the state of Collis's health during the next few weeks. He was so determined that the world should not know of his illness in case the news should damage him in some way, or result in his being 'dropped'. It was the first time in his life that he had been seriously ill and even now at his age he was reluctant publicly to admit to any physical frailty. In fact just before Christmas, Collis began to experience severe pains whenever he took a deep breath. Pain killers proved useless and he was again taken to hospital where he had two more operations. At last the pain eased and he was able to go home on Christmas Day, though in a very weak state.

On 20 January 1984 I heard from him again: 'I have turned the corner. Having not gone out of this house (except to hospital) for two months, I went down to the greenhouse this very day.'

By now Martin Jenkins at the BBC had selected the passages that he wanted to use and had put them all onto one tape. On 9 February I drove down to Abinger Common to play it over to Collis. It was a very fine winter's day and the sunshine was pouring through the French windows into the sitting-room where he sat looking frail but very cheerful. To my unmedical eye he seemed to have made a good recovery. Before lunch we listened with Irene to the tape and I was relieved to find that he liked it. His reaction in fact was the same as mine. We both felt that anyone who listened to it, knowing nothing of him previously, would find it interesting and out of the ordinary. In other words, it did manage to convey how unusual a man he was and how far outside the run of the sort of people normally to be heard talking on the radio.

Collis was very keen, over lunch, to know what was going on at the *Spectator* which had been plunged into turmoil a few days before by the sudden and unexpected dismissal of Alexander Chancellor by the new proprietor, Algy Cluff. I myself had resigned in protest and several others were talking of doing the same. Like everyone else Collis was baffled by Cluff's behaviour; but equally he disapproved of the resignations and before I left extracted a promise from me that I would continue to review books for the magazine if asked to do so. It is a promise I have kept.

He seemed confident that he was on the mend. Martin Jenkins had asked him if he would record some of his readings again. I suggested that the BBC could visit him at home but he was quite keen to go up to Broadcasting House in London and thought he would be fit enough to do this in a fortnight's time.

He told me that he had been visited by a faith healer, a woman, and was sure that he had benefited because he could feel the warmth in her fingers. 'Of course she has a lot of *theology* to go with it,' he said, 'but I don't accept any of that.' It was the only indication I had that as far as orthodox medicine was concerned, he was incurable. But he was, as usual, so confident and so vital that I went away sharing his optimism about his recovery.

About ten days later he rang me in the evening, his voice sounding faint. He said that he was very weak again and didn't think he would be able, after all, to do the readings. Would I do them instead? He died on 2 March 1984, aged eighty-four.

His funeral took place on 8 March at the little church at Abinger Common. Irene asked me to give a short address and also, if I liked, to read something from one of John's books.

When I took down *While Following the Plough* the book fell open at the following passage:

154

This field was on a considerable rise. I could see the village below me and a long way across the land. We plan our habitations, we design: and the result is sometimes good. Yet how often one is struck by the beauties that are undesigned, where there was no pre-arranged pattern, yet all is pattern. We planned the position of the Manor House; but we could not have hoped to arrange matters so that the red creeper would climb just to catch the last sunset ray, nor so arrange the growth of yellow flowers that they would lean against the high green field beyond. We planned the position of the church, but now it is locked in Nature's arm. I looked down and saw the double beauty of man's deliberations clothed in all the careless forms of earth.

More often I looked upwards at the great cathedral piles of cloud that passed along the winter sky, extravagant and erring shapes radiantly rimmed and quite ensilvered by the sun. Once, a broad shaft of light, let out from the clouds, beamed down upon the distant land. It lit up the ground on which it fell and slowly moved from field to field, from hedge to hedge, as if looking for something, like a giant search-light reversed. Then it went out suddenly as if switched off. The clouds above increased in splendour. Ah, it is a land, a land up there, that does belong to us though raised so high! Token of some great happiness that shall be fulfilled, the hope and promise written in every heart!

When the dusk fell and I could go on no longer, I often caught the sharp whiff of smell coming from the upturned earth. Scent is a mighty marvel. What it is I do not know. But I knew what this smell was, which is the most intoxicating of all. It was – Fertility: it was life itself coming across to me in pure sensation – the *odour* of eternal resurrection from the dead.

BOOKS BY JOHN STEWART COLLIS

Shaw (Jonathan Cape, 1925)
Forward to Nature (Jonathan Cape, 1927)
Farewell to Argument (Cassell, 1935)
The Sounding Cataract (Cassell, 1936)
An Irishman's England (Cassell, 1937)
While Following the Plough (Jonathan Cape, 1946)
Down to Earth (Jonathan Cape, 1947)
The Triumph of the Tree (Jonathan Cape, 1950)
The Moving Waters (Rupert Hart-Davis, 1955)
Paths of Light (Cassell, 1959)
An Artist of Life: Havelock Ellis (Cassell, 1959)
Marriage and Genius (Cassell, 1963)
Tolstoy: A Pictorial Biography (Burns and Oates, 1969)
Bound Upon a Course (Sidgwick and Jackson, 1971)
The Carlyles (Sidgwick and Jackson, 1972)
Christopher Columbus (Macdonald, 1976)
Living with a Stranger (Macdonald, 1978)

Compilations
The Vision of Glory (Charles Knight, 1972)
The Worm Forgives the Plough (Charles Knight, 1973)